BANGKOK
street food

BANGKOK
street food

TOM VANDENBERGHE & LUK THYS

Cooking and travelling in Thailand

LANNOO

Contents

Introduction

In recent years, the global interest in street food trends has grown enormously. So much so, that nowadays every self-respecting city in the world hosts at least one annual street food festival. There are few countries in the world however, where street food is as deeply rooted in the culture as in old Siam. Every day in Thailand millions of people, from all walks of life, will eat meals that are prepared at a food stall in the markets and on the streets; streets that are literally magically transformed into kitchens and restaurants, the pavements crammed with plastic chairs and fold up tables. Whereas we in the West think of pavements and roads to be used to walk on or to drive through, in Thailand the space is shared, and also used as a place to eat. At any hour of the day or night, in every kind of weather, armed with their food carts, an army of street sellers set up tables where ingredients are skilfully chopped, prepared, and served, then when they are done everything is tidied away again. It is hard to beat the sheer quantity and diversity of street food in Thailand, and the variety, abundance and quality of the ingredients cannot be matched anywhere in the world. These street cooks, with only the most basic cooking equipment, miraculously transform their ingredients into a huge array of tantalising dishes. If you really want to experience authentic Thai culture, then eating like the locals is the best way to do it, and you will also be rewarded with a vibrant and delicious eating experience.

In Thailand, eating out is commonplace and not unusual; in fact, it is something most people do at least once a day, just part of the daily social life. At any time of day you can find improvised mobile kitchens everywhere: plastic chairs on the side of a road, in a somewhat fancier restaurant, at a train station, on the beach, during a picnic in the park, on pretty much every street corner, under bridges... You can bet on it, they will be there. Wherever there are people, there will be someone cooking and the most fantastic dishes will be on offer. There is no better way to immerse yourself in the Thai ambiance than at a food market, where people come to meet, chat, eat and drink, and it is difficult to say which, if any, takes priority over the other.

Setting up a food stall on the street is often a safety net for those who find themselves without an income, sometimes immigrants or people who don't have a permanent job. There is the classic story of a widow who sets up a noodle stall in a desperate attempt to make ends meet; the business flourishes and after a couple of years she is able to move into a permanent restaurant, where fame of her aromatic noodle soup continues to grow. We also hear tell of the student who sells grilled pork sate sticks after school to pay for his studies, or of the migrant worker who makes and sells papaya salad to earn a bit extra, when rice planting season in the north east of Thailand has finished for the year.

In recent times there has been a marked rise in the standard of living in Thailand, the traditional markets are gradually being replaced by modern supermarkets, and street food stalls are making way for air conditioned eating halls. Stricter hygiene standards and a better, safer infrastructure are becoming the rule. Nevertheless the concept of eating street food is so popular and deeply rooted in Thai culture that it is hard to believe that Bangkok will ever become another Singapore, where food sellers are banned from the streets and eating centres are the norm. Many of the most famous Thai dishes were invented on one street corner or another, and grew from their humble origins to gastronomic heights. The heart and soul of Thai cuisine is on the street, waiting to be tried by anyone with a culinary thirst, or simply a hungry tummy.

The marketplace was historically the beating heart of the community, and the only place where you could go to buy your food. Canny stall holders and merchants saw an opportunity to offer their customers an even better service, and began to prepare take away meals. This however meant bringing their cooking utensils back and forth from home every day. Sometimes they would stop to serve a random client encountered on the way, and slowly the mobile kitchens evolved; instead of serving their customers in the market they brought, as it were, the market place to the people.

An explosion of street food culture in Thailand followed the influx of Chinese migrants. In their adopted homeland the new settlers slept together in large halls, but as no kitchen facilities were available in this type of accommodation, those who had some cooking experience, quickly began to set up in front of their lodgings, where they would prepare meals for the whole group.

The 'haph' a long wooden pole with a woven basket on each end, which looks rather like an old fashioned balance scale, is one of the oldest ways to transport and sell street food, and this historic way of selling food can still regularly be seen in Thailand today. The haph enabled the sellers to easily maneuver through narrow streets, over bridges and between the many market stalls, bringing their wares to the people wherever they may be, sometimes even bringing a few little chairs for their customers to sit on too.

Historically, the boat of course was also of great importance for transporting and delivering food. However the iconic floating markets, so often shown to depict the archetypal image of the kingdom of Thailand, have now become more of a tourist attraction. Many of the populated areas of Thailand developed close to the rivers and canals, due to the proximity of a supply of water, fish and a means of transport. There were also boats called 'kuaytiaw rua', which were fully equipped floating kitchens, from which noodle soup was prepared and sold to the residents living both on and next to the water. You can sometimes still see a boat in the window of a noodle seller's shop, where they keep their cooking utensils or ingredients, as a tribute to the traditional cooking boat.

More recently the bicycle has made inroads into the world of street food. Cycling from door to door the sellers would advertise their presence with their own unique jingles. These jingles could be anything from a ringing bell, knocking wood, to a sung melody, or a whistle, this meant that people no longer had to stand outside waiting for their favourite seller to go by.

The bicycle was quickly followed by motorised vehicles adding everything from motor bikes with side cars to modified pick-ups to the list of ways to deliver *Meals on wheels!*

About Tom

When I visited Bangkok for the first time in 1995, it was immediately apparent how cooking and everything to do with food are an integral part of life here, not only in the capital but throughout the whole country. It seemed as if life here completely revolved around enjoying one culinary activity or another. At any time of day or night it is possible to treat yourself to something to eat, from a simple snack to an extended complex meal, and for every stall that is closing for the day there is another one just opening up for business.

My passion for authentic Thai cuisine developed over time, and at first it took a bit of getting used to the real Thai food. Like many tourists, possibly nervous of hygiene or other issues, I ate in Thai restaurants that were adapted for Westerners, with a menu card in English on the table. At first I didn't dare eat from the food stalls on the street, but slowly step by step I became more adventurous. It has now become my favourite pastime and there isn't a single day when I am travelling, that I don't eat at food stalls on the street. In general my rule is to see where there are a lot of people gathered around a stall, as this means there is something special to taste.

After hundreds of experiments with Thai cooking in my own kitchen and a dozen culinary-inspired trips to every corner of the world, my then girlfriend and I, decided to give up our nine-to-five jobs and go and live in Thailand for a year. However great the temptation was to just go travelling, reading and lazing about for a year, we wanted to get more out of our sabbatical. Before we really realised it we were organising culinary trips to Thailand, Vietnam and Indonesia for groups from Belgium and the Netherlands.

Following our experience introducing many groups to Thai, then later Vietnamese food culture, we started our company Kookstudio Eetavontuur (Cooking studio Eating adventure) in Belgium. Our initial idea was based on the principle of the Thai street food sellers, as we wanted to share our knowledge of Thai cuisine and let our clients taste authentic dishes. No sooner said than done; we rented a building and built a cooking studio. Today Kookstudio Eetavontuur has grown into a successful cooking workshop and catering business.

I first met food photographer Luk Thys, the man behind 'Foodphoto' in 2005. Together we began drawing plans for a cook and travel book about street food more concrete. In 2009 we published our first cook and travel book together Bangkok. Together we have to date released four books: Bangkok, Hanoi, Singapore & Penang and New York. However, our wish list of street food destinations in as yet far from complete.

For the first time ever in Belgium, in 2011 and with Foodphoto as our logistical partner we organised a summer full of street food festivals. For three consecutive weekends everyone could have a taste of the street kitchens of various continents, which was subsequently followed by two more summers of festivals.

Following the publication of our most recent book, New York street food, and inspired by the city itself, I opened a noodle bar in my home town of Ghent. Noodle bar Ramen is now running at full steam thanks to the enthusiasm of the visitors and a wonderful team of staff.

About this book

We hope that this book will give you a least an insight into the street food culture of Thailand, and will also contribute to increasing the positive perception of street food in general. The recipes we offer have been updated, or are a continuation of those in our first publication. However this merely scrapes the surface, and we can only give you a glimpse into the never ending diversity of food on offer in the world of Thai cuisine. Not only is the subject vast, but is also in a state of continual evolution, with new dishes appearing and others disappearing all the time.

We were given some of the recipes by street sellers who were willing to share their secrets, others we developed ourselves through much experimentation. You should aim to cook like a Thai chef - they don't measure things out during cooking - and keep tasting. Don't be a slave to the given measurements; one chilli is not the same as another, sometimes a lime will tastes sourer, or a clove of garlic more intense than usual, and so forth. It is important to find the right balance of flavours between the five basic tastes: sweet, sour, salt, bitter, and spicy.

In 2013 and 2014 I visited New York, Tokyo, Berlin, Paris, Amsterdam and Brussels to sniff out the local street food scenes there. Since my first book about Bangkok street food was released, I have changed somewhat, evolving both as a passionate street eater but also as a chef. Visiting hundreds of food stalls and markets, big and small, has enriched my perceptions and broadened my view of this exciting world. The metropolis of Bangkok has changed since then too and following the perceptible global street food revolution that has been happening in the last few years, it was time for me to go back to Thailand, the place where it all began. Thailand is the place where my heart was won and my passionate appetite for street food took shape.

My new quest in search of the exciting stories of people and their dishes became an invigorating and delicious re-discovery of street food vendors, acquaintances and friends of old, renewing my wonderment and enriching my knowledge. Enjoy *Bangkok street food revisited!*

Locations

Street food is everywhere in Bangkok; under bridges and on markets, in train and bus stations and at festivals, even on pavements or on the grounds of the holy temples! Wherever there are people, there is cooking. To help you locate certain businesses and dishes easily, we have divided the book into several well-known and some less well-known street food regions. We zoom in on neighbourhoods and areas either with a high concentration, or an exceptional selection of street food on offer. But we also take you to places in the city which we think are certainly worth making an effort to visit for culinary and/or cultural reasons.

Bangkok is on the move. Travelling around Bangkok is still time consuming, can be tiring and sometimes frustrating, but the modern public transport system here is changing fast to try and catch up with demand. If you are in the wrong place at the wrong time you can get stuck for hours in a traffic jam, so by being conscious of your commute you can save yourself a lot of time. Try not to plan too much into your programme and take the time to get to know the areas you find the most interesting. The following parts of the city are extensively explored in this book: Thewet, Chinatown, historic Bangkok, the Chao Praya River and modern Bangkok. Have a great time on this culinary city trip!

In and around Thewet

To the North of the famous back packer's district, Khao San, Thewet is a charming, lively and traditional neighbourhood, conveniently situated near the Chao Praya Rivier. The pier at the end of the flower market is the ideal starting point for a traffic jam-free boat trip on the Chao Praya River Express Boat which connects the north and south of the city. Just to the east is the Dusit area. The West-loving king Rama V built his royal palace here and you will recognise the neighbourhood from the slightly European flavour of the architecture. You will either love or hate the Khao San area depending on how you feel about all those backpackers trooping around together. For me it is a bit of both, it is still a unique neighbourhood for travel information and for a night out.

Wat Thewarat is the central temple in Thewet and is an important one for the Thai royal family where Monks stride along the streets making their daily rounds. Surrounding the temple are many traditional wooden buildings some of which house university departments including amongst others the trainee chefs.

There is a lot to discover here for foodies, and you can certainly spend several days wondering around the awesome, authentic markets in the neighbourhood. There is no shortage of food stalls, where you can satisfy your hunger at any time of the day. But there are also plenty of gourmet restaurants in the area where you can taste some more refined Thai cuisine.

Chinatown

Neon light flooded Yawalat Road is the arterial route through Chinatown. It is a mecca for street food lovers in Bangkok and if you enjoy tradition and history, then this is the perfect neighbourhood to go and explore. The countless surrounding alleyways will reveal their culinary secrets bit by bit.

There is no other area of Bangkok with such a high concentration of street food on offer. You can eat around the clock and a visit in the early morning is a completely different experience to a visit in the evening. In this neighbourhood you can eat dishes that have been cooked by the same family for three generations while each individual market trader prepares a different dish, evoking their own unique ethos.

The Chinese immigrants relocated to this area at the end of the 18th century when they were thrown out of Rattanakosin when construction of the royal palace began. There is a history of clan wars in Chinatown, but nowadays it is the street vendors who compete with each other on the culinary scene.

Historic Bangkok

The historic island Rattankosin, is the area between the Chao Praya and the connecting canal to the east. In this part of town you will find many of the top tourist attractions including the Sanam Luang square, the royal palace, Wat Phra Keow, Wat Po, the city pillar, the amulet market and the national museum. More than ten thousand tourists visit these historical sites every day.

It is forbidden by law to sell street food around these holy locations, but more often than not the tourist hot-spots are not the best places to eat anyway. It is worth taking the trouble to walk the short distance to the richly diverse, authentic markets, Pak Khlong Talaad (the flower market), the amulet market and the Siriraj market, which are busy and bustling. Or try the Sam Phreang neighbourhood where it is like taking a trip back through 70 years of culinary history.

Modern Bangkok

Modern Bangkok is a bustling world of chic shopping centres, top-end food courts and food markets, modern blocks of flats, roof-top bars, and high end hotels. Whatever you can think of you will find it here. Modern Bangkok is difficult to delineate, the city is so dynamic and so huge that it is almost impossible to say exactly where it begins or where it ends. Amongst others there are the business districts to the south of the Chao Praya River, the consular districts in Silom and Sathorn, the hyper modern shopping district Sukhumvit and the trendy new neighbourhoods like Ari and Thong Lo.

The highly efficient skytrain (BTS) and the underground (MRT) connect to all parts of the city. The speed with which Bangkok is evolving is the reason for the marked differences and is what makes this city so fascinating. The contrast between the provincial feeling of the Khlong Toey market and the chic Siam Paragon Plaza is almost shocking, but is part of the charm of the irrepressible and ever-changing Bangkok.

Getting reacquainted with Thewet

Hungry for an exciting new street food adventure, as well as an enormous bowl of fresh noodles, I arrive at Suvarnabhumi Airport just outside Bangkok. I head to the underground platform to wait for the first skytrain that will take me to the centre. For a mere 50 baht (€1.50) and travelling at breakneck speed, within 20 minutes I disembark at Paya Thai station in the middle of Bangkok. It is at this point I truly leave the speed and comfort of airport transport, including buses and taxis, far behind me. Outside I find a motorbike taxi, and with my small rucksack, hop on for the last two kilometres of my journey. A few minutes later I am standing in the reception of the guest house. This feels like coming home, I breathe in the familiar smells, the heat is overwhelming. I am back in Thewet. Let the eating party begin!

For years I have used the Taewez Guesthouse as a base camp for my culinary explorations through South East Asia. In this cosy neighbourhood the people are friendly and the food is fantastic. Thewet is close to one of the oldest and most authentic markets in Bangkok, and it seems as if not much has changed. Everything is still gently going on as it was before, business as usual in the relaxed atmosphere that I love, life in Thewet is buzzing. In contrast to the Chao Praya River, it quietly wends its way, until you reach central point, the market! Beginning early, around four o'clock in the morning, it is bustling with activity.

I love getting up with the sun and luckily for me, in Thailand the days begin very early. The quality of light at this time of day is really tender and almost theatrically beautiful. Though comparatively quiet, there is still plenty to watch on the streets as the day begins. My morning coffee is sacred, so the first thing I do is go and get a cup in the coffee house/internet café, across the road from the guest house. While I am enjoying a strong espresso, I read the latest news in the *Bangkok Post*, sitting back between a cash point and a public weighing scale. The lady running the coffee house is the perfect remedy if you got out of bed on the wrong side, eccentric but also generous Pi Suyad is always in a good mood. Even if I haven't been there for a while – because I have been travelling or back in Belgium – every time she welcomes me with a heartfelt greeting, *sabai dee mai, khun Tom* (How are you, Mr. Tom?) and kindly offers me toast and cake to go with my coffee.

Taking a walk down the street I find a stall selling **coconut puddings** (*khanom khlok*) and decide to buy some. These are, without a doubt, one of my favourite breakfast dishes and in my opinion the perfect accompaniment to a strong cup of coffee. At the next stall, I recognise a lady I came across on a previous visit, still selling her **Thai dim sum** (*khanom jeep*) and on the opposite side of the road another familiar face, another khanom khlok-chef. Though 10 years have gone by, I am pleased to see that the same sellers are still going strong, still standing in the same spot as they were, every day apart from weekends, when there are fewer people at the Thewet market, and on a Monday, when they clean the pavements. It is sometimes said that the 'khanom khlok' makers are very patient and friendly people, perhaps because you have to be a very patient kind of person to make the dish, as it does takes a while before it is ready.

At day break the barefoot Buddhist monks, in their saffron red robes leave the Wat Thewalat temple to collect alms on the streets. The woman, on the stall next to the coconut puddings seller, is cooking **grilled pork sate** (*moo yang*) and grilled meat balls, and she offers food to the monks, at the same time showing her respect with the traditional 'wai' greeting.

Placing the palms of your hands together, with the fingers pointing upwards, while keeping your hands close to the chest, mouth or head and slightly bowing your head and body, the 'wai' greeting is the Thai equivalent of a handshake. The higher the status of the person you are greeting, or the more respect you want to show, the higher your hands should be. It makes me so happy to get reacquainted with this neighbourhood, *Sawatdee Thewet*!

Coconut puddings
ขนมครก
khanom khlok

Khlok is the Thai word for 'mortar' a descriptive name indicating the shape of this delicious snack.

Ingredients

350 ml thick coconut cream
50 g + 1 tbsp. sugar
2 and ½ tbsp. tapioca flour
400 g rice flour
50 g fresh coconut pulp,
crushed finely in a mortar
3 tbsp. uncooked rice,
crushed finely in a mortar
2 tsp. salt
750 ml light coconut milk
2 tbsp. vegetable oil

Filling

1 spring onion, sliced in rings
or kernels from 1 cob
of sweet corn

- Put the thick coconut cream together with 50 g of sugar into a saucepan. Allow the sugar to melt and leave to cool. When cool, add the tapioca flower. Set aside. Combine the rice flour with the crushed coconut pulp; add the ground rice, salt and 1 tablespoon of sugar. Stir and mix with the light coconut milk.
- Grease in the 'khanom khlok' pan with some oil and heat on a medium gas stove. Wait a few seconds and spoon in the rice mixture with the light coconut milk until about ⅔ full. Immediately add a dab of the sweet thick coconut cream mixture over the top. Sprinkle some spring onion or some corn kernels on top. Cover it with a lid and leave to cook for a few minutes or until the puddings are firm.
- Remove the puddings gently with a spoon. Put two halves on top of each other and serve warm.

Clean the 'khanom khlok' pan with oil.

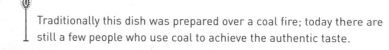

Traditionally this dish was prepared over a coal fire; today there are still a few people who use coal to achieve the authentic taste.

Thai dim sum
ขนมจีบ
khanom jeep

If you like a small savory snack in the morning, healthy and not greasy, try dim sum. Just point to show which ones you want to buy.

Dim sum

2 dried mushrooms
(e.g. cloud ear, shiitake)
350 g prawns, peeled, deveined and chopped
250 g minced pork
1 tsp. ginger, chopped
1 spring onion, chopped
1 shallot, chopped
20 wonton skins
1 tbsp. oyster sauce
1 tsp. Chinese rice wine
1 tsp. sesame oil
½ tsp. sugar

Sauce

2 tbsp. light soy sauce
2 tbsp. dark soy sauce
1 tbsp. rice vinegar
1 pinch of salt
1 pinch of sugar

- Soak the mushrooms in water for 15 minutes, drain and squeeze out the excess liquid. Chop finely.
- Combine prawns, pork, mushrooms, ginger, spring onion and shallot and mix well. Add the oyster sauce, rice wine, sesame oil and sugar and mix well.
- Place 2 teaspoons of this mixture in the middle of a wonton skin.
- Fold up the sides to form a cup-like shape. If necessary, cut off any excess wonton skin. You must be able to see the filling. Repeat for the rest.
- Steam the dim sum for about 5-10 minutes (according to their filling), until cooked. In the meantime, mix all the ingredients for the sauce. Serve the dim sum with the sauce.

Different fillings are possible. When you see white dim sum, rice paper has been used instead of wonton skins.

:⚬: — *Grilling*
ยาง

Grilled pork
หมูย่าง/หมูปิ้ง
moo yang / moo ping

It's the marinade that gives the pork a tender, savoury taste. Some of the 'moo yang' vendors sell the pork without the skewers cut in slices on a plate but adding some cucumber and fresh herbs, more as a side dish.
It goes really well with green papaya salad and some sticky rice.

Makes 10 pieces

10 wooden or bamboo skewers
400 g pork fillet, cut in thin strips
2 garlic cloves, chopped
6 coriander roots, scraped and chopped
½ tbsp. white ground pepper
4 tbsp. fish sauce
1 tbsp. light soy sauce
125 ml coconut cream
1 tbsp. vegetable oil
1 tbsp. caster sugar

Soak the skewers in water for 1 hour to prevent from burning.

Combine all the ingredients but the pork in a large mixing bowl, mix well. Let the pork strips marinate in this mixture for at least half an hour.

'Weave' the strips of pork onto the skewers and grill over charcoal for about 5 minutes, until cooked. Turn frequently.

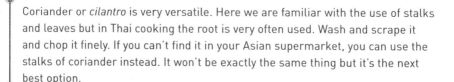

Coriander or *cilantro* is very versatile. Here we are familiar with the use of stalks and leaves but in Thai cooking the root is very often used. Wash and scrape it and chop it finely. If you can't find it in your Asian supermarket, you can use the stalks of coriander instead. It won't be exactly the same thing but it's the next best option.

Lunch time in Thewet

I spend the hours before lunch wandering through the market. Sitting on the corner are the egg peelers; this family takes the shells off three thousand eggs per day. A little further up the street the ice cube factory is running at full tilt, the workers cut the large blocks of ice into smaller pieces, which are then made into crushed ice to be used by the market traders and food stall holders in the neighbourhood. On the bridge over the canal and on the way to the pier fish are spread out on on wooden mats, and chillies are drying in round, reed rice baskets. The lady who works in the traditional Thai massage house, where I often used to visit, remembers me and comes over for a chat.

Around midday I start to walk back in the direction of the guest house; on the way, I check to see if Khun Nee is already open for business, but she is not there yet. Kuhn Nee runs a dtam sang restaurant, which means that the cooks prepare everything to order and you can choose what you want from the available ingredients. Among the classics on the menu are **stir-fried chicken with holy basil** (*gai phat krapao*) and **stir-fried pork with garlic and black pepper** (*moo kratiem phrik thai*) all, of course, are served with rice. Or a **spicy squid salad** (*yam pla muek*). If you want you can pep these dishes up with a dressing of fish sauce and chilli peppers (*naam pla phrik*), which is the liquid, Thai equivalent of salt and pepper in the West, a seasoning that is available everywhere.

The market place is being completely renovated. A new concrete floor is being put in and the whole place is being disinfected. The snooker table and bar that stood in the middle of the market place, where I spent many nights playing endless games of billiards with the locals, are being dismantled. Walking around the corner of the Samsen Road I reach the building of the national bank. It is here that I meet another lady who is preparing *khao soy gai* or **Chiang Mai curry noodles with chicken**. She tells me that she is originally from Chang Mai but that she has been in Bangkok for more than 30 years running a small eating house. She also tells me in confidence that Khun Nee has chosen another direction in her life, and a cheerful young woman has taken over her restaurant and is now making similar dishes. It is a shame. Khun Nee was enormously talented, preparing her dishes on her little gas burner, but that is how it goes. Time does not stand still; some businesses stay, others disappear. With two hands she passes me the noodle soup. I go and take a seat and squeeze lime juice over the creamy curry sauce and tuck in. Noodles are available in abundance in Thailand and are perfect for lunch.

— *Stir-Frying*
ผัด

Stir-fried chicken with holy basil on rice
ไก่ผัดกะเพรา
gai phat krapao

Ingredients

2 tbsp. vegetable oil
2 garlic cloves, crushed
250 g chicken breasts, boned and chopped in small pieces
2 big red chillies, chopped finely
2 bunches of holy basil (*bai krapao*)
2 tbsp. fish sauce
1 tbsp. sugar
2 tbsp. water or chicken stock

Heat the wok on medium heat. Add oil and garlic, stir-fry for a few seconds.
Turn up the heat and add the chicken. Add chilli and half of the basil.
Stir-fry for 1 minute, add fish sauce, sugar and water or stock. Turn down the heat to low. Add the rest of the basil, stir-fry for a few seconds and serve on rice.

You could also use pork instead of chicken.

There are three types of Thai basil. The two most frequently used are Thai basil (*bai horapa*) and holy basil (*bai krapao*). Bai horapa has a distinctive aniseed taste and is used in salads and curries. Bai krapao has a peppery flavour and is used in stir-fries. The third type is less common: lemon basil (*bai maenglak*). It has a sweet lemon taste, used in salads and soups and for adding fragrance to foods.

◊ — *Stir-Frying*
ผัด

Stir-fried pork with garlic and black pepper

หมูกระ เทียมพริกไทย

moo kratiem phrik thai

Ingredients

250 g pork fillet
1 garlic clove
15 white peppercorns
2 coriander roots, scraped and chopped
2 tbsp. vegetable oil
2 tbsp. fish sauce
2 tbsp. water or chicken stock
¼ tbsp. sugar
1 tsp. crushed pepper
1 handful coriander leaves
1 fried egg (optional)

Cut the pork into bite-size pieces.
Make a smooth paste from the garlic, white peppercorns and coriander roots, using a pestle and mortar.
Heat the wok on a low heat. Add oil and stir-fry the paste for 30 seconds. Add the pork and turn up the heat.
Add fish sauce, water or stock and sugar and keep stirring until pork is cooked.
Season this with the crushed pepper and garnish with coriander leaves.

Variations are possible with beef or prawns. When using meat, serve with steamed rice, some slices of cucumber and a fried egg, sunny-side-up on top.

◌ — **Boiling**
ต้ม

Spicy squid salad
ยำปลาหมึก

yam pla muek

Forget chewy, rubbery deep-fried squid or calamari we get served on
our plates far too often. This blanched squid melts like butter and the
simplicity of this dish, combined with the spicy freshness, is astonishing.

Salad

200 g fresh squid, cleaned
and cut in strips or rings
1 sweet white onion, finely sliced
2 kaffir lime leaves,
very finely sliced (optional)
1 stalk of lemon grass, white part
sliced finely
10 mint leaves
8 coriander leaves (optional)
8 flat parsley leaves or Chinese
celery leaves, shredded
1 small tomato, quartered
1 tbsp. rice vinegar

Dressing

2-4 small red and green
chillies, chopped very finely
3 tbsp. lime juice
2 tbsp. fish sauce
1 pinch of sugar

Combine all the ingredients for the dressing and
taste. It should taste sour, salty and spicy. Bring
some salted water with ricevinegar to the boil
and blanch the squid briefly. As soon as the squid
changes from transparent to opaque, remove from
the water. Put in iced water to stop the cooking
process and keep aside. Gently combine the other
ingredients for the salad, add the squid, pour over
the dressing and serve immediately.

The squid can be replaced by other ingredients,
like grilled beef, grilled prawns, crispy pork,
seared tuna, etc. This is the basic recipe for a
'yam', a Thai salad. The distinctive quality about
this recipe is that sweet onion is used instead of
shallots. Usually, shallots are used in a 'yam' but
the softer, sweet taste of the onion works very well
with the delicate taste of the blanched squid.

This is one of the kicks of Thai cuisine: the sourness of the lime, combined
with the heat of the chillies and the freshness of the herbs lift this dish up
to a higher level. It is highly addictive and will make you want to beg for more!

Chiang Mai Chicken

ข้าวซอยไก่

kao soi gai

This is a wonderful complete meal, in which the deep-fried noodles contrast exceptionally well with the smooth texture of the soup.

Noodles and chicken

2 chicken legs
4 tbsp. coconut cream
1 tbsp. palm sugar
2 tbsp. light soy sauce
1 tsp. dark soy sauce
500 ml chicken stock
1 handful of fresh egg noodles
a few deep-fried egg noodles
2 spring onions, chopped
1 handful of chopped
coriander leaves

Paste

3 large, red, dried chillies,
deseeded, soaked in water for
10 minutes, drained, chopped
2 red shallots, chopped
1 tsp. coriander seeds, toasted
2 garlic cloves, chopped
2 cm turmeric, chopped
2 cm ginger, chopped
3 coriander roots, scraped and
chopped
1 pinch of salt

To serve with

pickled vegetables
1 shallot, sliced finely
1 lime, cut in wedges

Pound the paste ingredients together, using a pestle and mortar, until smooth. Warm the coconut cream in a pan until the oil starts to separate. Turn down the heat and add the paste. Fry the paste in the oil for 5 minutes. Add the chicken and simmer. Season with palm sugar, light and dark soy sauce. Moisten with stock and simmer for about 20 minutes, the chicken should be cooked.

Blanch the egg noodles, put into a bowl, top with the chicken and pour over the soup.

Top it with deep-fried egg noodles and garnish with spring onion and coriander. Serve with pickled vegetables, slices of shallot and wedges of lime.

You can find variations on this dish (for instance with beef) but never with pork as originally it is a Muslim dish.

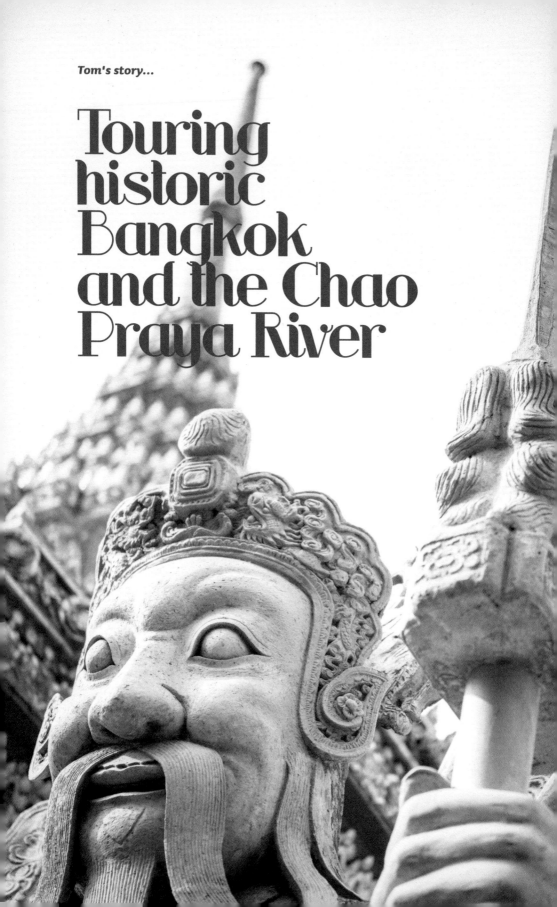

Touring historic Bangkok and the Chao Praya River

There are many good reasons to have your base in Thewet, but one fantastic advantage is the proximity to one of the stops of the Chao Phraya River Express Boat. From six o'clock in the morning to seven in the evening these boats sail up and down the Chao Phraya River, and in my opinion, it is the best and most pleasurable way to get around in Bangkok. A refreshing breeze, no traffic jams, and meanwhile you can sit back and enjoy the view, and watch the life on the river banks as you sail by. On the skyline you will catch a glimpse of some of the significant buildings, sites such as Wat Po, Wat Arun and the royal palace. Every time I take this boat trip, I am still overcome by an intense feeling of freedom and happiness.

On these regular morning boat rides, one of my favourite places to stop off is Pak Khlong Talaat, the flower market to the north of the Memorial Bridge, which is one of the wholesale markets in the city. I thoroughly enjoy just strolling around and soaking up the atmosphere, even just doing a bit of window shopping is an experience. The quality of the products here is unbelievable and the sheer abundance of fruit, vegetables, flowers and plants takes your breath away. After a wander I treat myself to a cup of warm soya milk (*naam tahuu*) and a few **Thai donuts** (*pah tong koh*), and on the stall next to this I see people eating portions of **khanom jeen rice noodles with curry**.

It is only nine o'clock in the morning but already very warm outside. I carry on walking up to Wat Po, where I love to treat myself to a massage by the students at the Wat Po massage school. On the way I see a young girl steaming several different sorts of potatoes, and a bunch of fresh soya beans hangs from her steaming basket. Around Wat Po there are many shops selling medicinal herbs and a whole array of food stalls offering food with heath giving properties. After a relaxing massage it is time for a real breakfast of **rice porridge** (*joak*). I happily pull up a chair, while the man next to me orders **tofu with minced pork** (*toa huu throing kreang*). In Asia it is not uncommon to combine what we think of as vegetarian ingredients with meat. The various cuisines are not so easily divided into separate categories. After breakfast I saunter on past the Royal Palace and so reach the amulet market, where they sell necklaces with images of Buddha. Many Thai people are constantly searching for that one talisman that will bring them luck or protect them from the forces of evil.

🔥 — **Deep-Frying**
ทอด

Thai donuts
ปาท่องโก๋

pah thong koh

A couple in love is like *pah thong koh*.
An expression meaning that the parts are hard to split.

Ingredients

¼ tsp. bicarbonate of soda
1 tsp. baking powder
1 tsp. sugar
1 pinch of salt
200 ml water
600 g flour
1 tbsp. vegetable oil
oil for deep-frying

- Mix bicarbonate of soda with baking powder, sugar and salt.
- Add water and flour. Stir well. Add vegetable oil and cover with a kitchen towel. Leave for 4 hours at room temperature.
- Heat the oil for deep-frying.
- Sprinkle some flour on a work surface.
- Take a handful of dough and make 2 rectangles (1,5cm x 6cm). Stick them together to form a cross shape with a bit of water.
- Deep-fry until golden and crispy.
- Drain and serve.

Recently the coffee industry has boomed in Thailand with Starbucks and the like. Thai people have picked up on the popularity of good coffee and have started to serve a real espresso, frothy cappuccino or a mellow latte. When you find a coffee stall, chances are high that a pah thong koh-vendor is around. Sometimes *pah thong koh* is served with rice soup (*khao tom* or *johk*). Shred it to pieces and dip it in the soup.

Khanom is actually the Thai word for dessert, but can also mean 'dough'. There are so many different variations of khamom jeen recipes, that you could in fact devote an entire book to them alone. The most well-known of these are *khanom jeen sao nam* (khanom jeen noodles with coconut and pineapple), *khanom jeen nam ya* (khanom jeen with fish and wild ginger) and *khanom jeen namngiao* (khanom jeen with met Burmese curry and pigs blood).

◐ — *Stir-Frying*
ผัด

Khanom jeen
noodles with green curry and fish
ขนมจีนแกงเขียวหวานปลา

khanom jeen gaeng kiaw warn pla

Noodles and curry; a very rich dish with many local variations.
Here below is a simple and accessible version of the recipe.

Noodles and fish

4 tbsp. coconut cream (the thick layer
from the top of a can of coconut milk)
2 tbsp. fish sauce
½ tsp. sugar
3 Thai aubergine, chopped
200 ml coconut milk
300 g firm white fish, preferably monkfish
or catfish, cut into strips
200 ml chicken stock
4 kaffir lime leaves, vein removed and shredded
1 handful Thai basil
500 g white khanom jeen rice noodles

Green curry paste

12 bird's eye chillies, roughly chopped
2 large green chillies, roughly chopped
2 shallots, finely chopped
2 garlic cloves, finely chopped
1 lemongrass stem, only the bottom white part,
finely chopped
2 slices galanga (Thai ginger), finely chopped
1 coriander root, finely chopped
1 kaffir lime leaf, vein removed, finely chopped
1 krachai root (Chinese ginger), finely chopped
1 tsp. shrimp paste, toasted in aluminium foil
1 tsp. coriander seeds, toasted
½ tsp. cumin seeds, toasted
1 tsp. white peppercorns

In a pestle and mortar grind all the ingredients for the curry paste together to form
a smooth consistency. Keep to one side.
Warm a wok over a high heat. Put the
coconut cream in and stir until the fat is
released, then turn the heat down as low
as possible; add 2 or 3 tablespoons of the
curry paste. Fry the curry paste off over
a low heat for a few minutes. Season with
the fish sauce and add sugar to taste.
Add in the aubergine and continue to stir-fry
for 30 seconds. Add the coconut milk and the
fish strips and gently bring to the boil. Pour
in the chicken stock and bring back to the
boil. Finally add the kaffir lime leaves and
the Thai basil.
Cook the khanom jeen noodles, according
to the instructions on the packet and serve
with a garnish of fresh soya bean shoots,
sliced cucumber and a sprigs of coriander.

For garnish

handful of fresh soya bean shoots
slices of cucumber
fresh coriander sprigs

💧 — **Boiling** 💧 — **Steaming**
ต้ม   นึ่ง

Rice porridge
โจ๊ก

joak

A favourite amongst Thai people, a hearty breakfast or a filling,
yet digestible, late night snack.

Ingredients

200 g (broken) rice
1 l chicken stock
100 g minced pork
3 tbsp. light soy sauce
¼ tsp. ground white pepper
2 hardboiled eggs, quartered
2 spring onions, chopped
1 handful coriander leaves
1 tbsp. deep-fried garlic
1-3 large chillies
200 ml vinegar
extra fish sauce

Rinse the rice a few times with cold water. Cook
the rice using any method. Bring stock to the boil.
For extra flavour you can add Chinese celery,
bruised lemongrass, cracked white peppercorns,
coriander root, galangal, etc. Add the rice and
simmer briefly. Some people prefer a more porridge-
like consistency, others a firmer texture of the rice.
Simmer accordingly. Season it with soy sauce
and pepper.

Portion out the egg quarters in the serving bowls,
spoon over the soup and finish with coriander, spring
onion and garlic. Serve immediately with a small dish
of chillies in vinegar, an extra bowl of fish sauce to
season and accompaniments to your liking.

Other accompaniments could be grated fresh
ginger, peanuts, deep-fried fish, dried shrimp or
dried fish, roasted pork, raw egg yolk, stir-fried
prawns, chicken, pickled vegetables, etc.

You can cook the rice in the stock, adding extra
water or stock if necessary. Broken rice has a nuttier
flavour, a firmer and stickier texture than 'whole' rice.

In earlier times this porridge was prepared in the
evening and simmered all night on a very low heat.

Tofu, minced pork and Chinese celery

บะหมี่เกี๊ยวปู

toa huu throing kreang

Though some people may find it strange to use tofu and pork in the same dish, it is not uncommon to find this combination in Chinese cuisine. The Chinese celery and Thai chilli give this dish a fresh, powerful and unmistakably Thai character.

Ingredients

2 tbsp. vegetable oil
1 garlic clove, crushed
1 red Thai chilli, in rings
200 g pork, minced
200 ml water
1 tbsp. light soy sauce
1 tbsp. oyster sauce
¼ tsp sugar
200 g extra firm yellow Chinese tofu, cut into 2cm cubes (or deep fry a less firm tofu until golden brown)
3 sticks Chinese celery, leaves and stalks, roughly chopped
¼ tsp. ground white pepper

Warm a wok over medium heat. Add the oil, garlic and chilli and stir-fry for a few seconds. Add the minced pork, turn up the heat and continue to stir-fry until the meat is nicely browned and separated.

Pour in the 200ml water and allow to cook through for 1 minute. Season with the soy sauce, oyster sauce and sugar, and stir well.

Add the tofu and allow to warm through. Add in the Chinese celery and continue to gently cook for one minute. Finish with a pinch of ground white pepper and serve with rice.

You can substitute the pork with any number of other ingredients for example beef or chicken. For full-time vegetarians you can use quorn or finely chopped mushrooms, and the oyster sauce can be replaced with a vegetarian mushroom sauce.

Street food on the river bank

If you are coming from the direction of Tha Phra Chan, the river side restaurants – on the right hand side – are the ideal place to stop and take a break, have a tasty snack or lunch, or simply enjoy the fascinating view.

From under their aluminium roofs, some of the eating houses you find here will be serving **crispy fish and green mango salad** (*yam pla duk foo*). This is definitely one of my favourite dishes and a good illustration of the perfect balance between yin and yang. The slippery texture of the sour green mango in a fresh spicy dressing of lime and chilli, in combination with the crunchy fried fish and peanuts, is a real winner!

I still have vivid memories of ten years ago, when Eva and I often ate in one or other of the restaurants along the river bank, restaurants which offer a bit of everything. We would talk for hours as we enjoyed the view and the cooling breeze. I remember it as if it was only yesterday. As a starter we would share a portion of **grilled chicken satay** (*satay gai*) with a delicious peanut sauce, followed by **Chinese broccoli with crispy pork** (*phat pak kanaa*) and a wonderful **hot and sour soup with prawns** (*tom yam kung*). It is often the case that my clearest memories, those that I can bring most easily to mind, revolve around food. And is it just me, or does a meal really taste just a little bit better when you share it with someone you care about?

Behind the pier of the Siriraj hospital (Tha Wang Lang or Siriraj Pier) is a culinary oasis. To get to the neighbourhood of this famous food paradise I take the ferry and cross over the river to the Chang Pier. Wandering through the narrow streets I am surrounded by countless food stalls and it is difficult to take in everything they have on offer. **Steamed fishcakes** (*ha mok pla*), **deep-fried spring rolls** (*poh piah thod*) and **steamed mackerel** (*pla tuu*) – and that is just the beginning, a fraction of what is on offer waiting to be bought and eaten.

Crispy fish and green mango salad
ยำปลาดุกฟู
yam pla duk foo

It's a missed opportunity that a lot of Thai restaurants abroad don't put this dish on their menus. Hard to understand because the unusual combination of textures and flavours is totally thrilling and is on the verge of perfection.

Crispy fish

1 catfish, sea bass or sea bream
1 smoked trout
1 large pinch of salt
oil for deep-frying

Dressing

3 tbsp. lime juice
2-4 small chillies, chopped finely
2 tbsp. fish sauce
1 tbsp. sugar

Green mango salad

1 small green mango
2 shallots, sliced finely
1 handful of roasted
or deep-fried peanuts
1 handful of mint leaves
1 handful of coriander leaves
2 deep-fried dried large chillies
(optional, for garnishing)

Preheat the oven to 190°C. Clean the fish (scale and remove the gut) and pat dry with kitchen paper. Dry the fish in the oven, this can take up to an hour, and then allow to cool. Fillet the fish.

In a food processor blitz together the fish, smoked trout and salt, but be careful not to let the crumbs get too fine, otherwise they won't stick together properly later.

Heat the oil and deep-fry a handful of the fish crumb mixture. When the bubbling foam dies down, bring the fish together with a slotted spoon, to form a sponge-like cluster. Flip the whole thing over and continue to fry until you have a beautifully golden brown patty. Allow to drain well on kitchen paper.

Bring the oil back up to temperature and repeat the process until you have used up all the fish crumbs.

Mix all the ingredients for the dressing together well.

Peel the mango and grate the flesh, then mix it with the shallots, peanuts, mint and coriander, and place onto a serving dish. Arrange the deep-fried fish patties on top and the large chillies if you are using them. Pour over the dressing and serve immediately.

At the market, the three main components of this salad (crispy fish, mango salad and dressing) are sold separately.

◐ — *Grilling*
ยาง

Grilled chicken or pork satay

สะเต๊ะไก่/สะเต๊ะหมู

satay gai / moo

Satay is always served with peanut sauce and cucumber relish. Sometimes more elaborate versions are seen, with pineapple or cherry tomato.

Makes 10 pieces

10 wooden or bamboo skewers
450 g chicken or pork fillet
2 tsp. coriander seeds
½ tsp. cumin seeds
2 garlic cloves, chopped
4 red shallots, chopped
2-5 cm fresh ginger
2-5 cm turmeric root
1 tsp. salt
2 tbsp. vegetable oil
2 tbsp. white caster sugar

Soak the skewers in water for 1 hour; this will prevent burning while grilling.

Cut the chicken or pork into fine strips.

Using a pestle and mortar, pound the coriander seeds, cumin, garlic, shallot, ginger, turmeric until smooth. Add salt, oil and sugar. Let chicken or pork marinate in this mixture for at least 1 hour.

'Weave' the strips of meat on the skewers and grill, turning regularly.

Turmeric, also known as yellow root or curcuma is a member of the ginger family and not, as sometimes mistakenly thought, related to saffron. Hiding under the thick brown skin is a deep orange coloured spice. When it is added to food, it gives the dish an orange colour, which explains the confusion with saffron, however they are not interchangeable and you can't replace one with the other.

Turmeric has been used since time immemorial in herbal remedies. The list of diseases and illnesses, for which turmeric plays a healing or preventative role is a long one, but it is most commonly used as an anti-inflammatory. Despite the undoubted healing properties of the root, it is a tricky ingredient in your kitchen, because of the stubborn stains it leaves behind. Wear gloves when you are peeling the turmeric root to prevent your fingers from turning yellow.

Chinese broccoli with crispy pork

ผัดผักคะน้าหมูกรอบ

phat pak kanaa moo khrob

The bitter taste of the vegetables combines magnificently with the salty, crispy pork.

Ingredients

1 tbsp. vegetable oil
1 garlic clove, crushed
1 small chilli, cut finely (optional)
2 stalks of Chinese broccoli, cut diagonally
2 tbsp. oyster sauce
1 tbsp. fish sauce
½ tsp. sugar
4 tbsp. water or light chicken stock
10 cm crispy pork, cut in bite-sized pieces
¼ tsp. freshly ground black pepper

Put the wok on medium heat. When warm, add vegetable oil, garlic and chilli when using. Stir-fry for a few seconds.
Add the Chinese broccoli, turn up the heat and stir-fry for 1 minute.
Add oyster sauce, fish sauce and sugar, keep stir-frying for another minute.
Add water or chicken stock, stir-fry for half a minute and turn down the heat.
Add crispy pork and finish with pepper.

Hot and sour soup with prawns

ต้มยำกุ้ง

tom yam kung

Tom means 'to boil' in Thai and *yam* 'to mix'.

Ingredients

8 prawns
1 l water
1 tbsp. *phrik pao* paste
3 tbsp. lime juice
2-4 stalks of lemon grass, bruised
6 slices galangal
8 kaffir lime leaves, shredded
2 shallots, sliced
2 garlic cloves
2 tbsp. fish sauce
1 handful straw or oyster mushrooms, chopped roughly
2-4 small chillies
1 handful cherry tomatoes, halved
1 handful saw leaf herb (*pak chee farang*) shredded or coriander leaves, chopped
1 spring onion, chopped

Remove heads (if there) and legs of the prawns. Shell the prawns, leaving the tail intact. Make a small incision along the back of the prawn and remove the black intestinal tract. Keep the shells and heads for making the stock.

Bring water with shells and heads to the boil for 15 minutes. Or for a richer stock, fry the shells and heads in a bit of oil, then add water. Strain and keep the liquid. Mix the phrik pao paste with the lime juice and set aside.

Add lemon grass, galangal, kaffir lime leaves, shallots, garlic and fish sauce to the stock and bring to the boil. Add mushrooms and keep simmering for 2 minutes. Add the prawns; once they turn pink, they are cooked. Turn off the heat. Add chilli and cherry tomatoes.

Put 1 teaspoon of the phrik pao-lime mixture in each bowl, pour over the soup and garnish with the saw leaf herb or coriander leaves and spring onion.

Whenever I catch a cold in Thailand - yes, it is possible to catch a cold in tropical weather! - I opt for 'tom yam kung'. Due to its immunity-boosting ingredients it works miracles.

Lemon grass, galangal and kaffir lime leaves give this soup its distinctive flavour. You can find this holy trinity bundled together, at most markets in Thailand. Be careful though, you are not supposed to eat these herbs!

According to several surveys concerning the popularity of Thai food around the world, 'tom yam kung' is listed as number 1 in the top 10 favourite Thai dishes. Equally, Thai people love this spicy soup and consider this one of their national dishes.

This soup should be eaten piping hot. It is often served in a kind of steamboat under which burning charcoals keep this soup hot during the meal. The freshness of the ingredients is crucial in preparing a perfect 'tom yam'. By adding the lime juice at the end, it preserves its fresh flavour.

This soup is often eaten ladled over a bowl of rice. But you may want to eat it just as a soup. There are variations, with mixed seafood (*tom yam thaleh*), chicken (*tom yam gai*) and fish (*tom yam pla*) available. Some cooks add (evaporated) milk or coconut milk at the end of the preparation to give it a creamier texture.

◊ — **Deep-Frying**
ทอด

Deep-fried spring rolls
ปอเปี๊ยะทอด

poh piah thod

Originally of Chinese-Vietnamese origin but Thai people adopted this golden snack eagerly. It's now widely available in Thailand.

Ingredients

100 g mung bean noodles
8 dried cloud ear mushrooms
200 g minced pork
2 garlic cloves, chopped
2 tbsp. fish sauce
2 tbsp. light soy sauce
½ tsp. sugar
½ tsp. ground white pepper
1 carrot, julienned
1 handful of soy bean sprouts
6 sheets of rice paper
(square or round, small size)
oil for deep-frying

Pour boiling water over the mung bean noodles, cover and let them rest for 3-4 minutes. Drain well and set aside.

Soak the dried mushrooms for 10 minutes in warm water and slice finely. Combine minced pork with garlic, fish sauce, soy sauce, sugar and pepper. Add mung bean noodles, mushrooms, carrot and soy bean sprouts.

Take a large bowl with warm water and put 1 rice paper in for a few seconds until soft.

Place a little bit of the mixture in the middle, fold one side over, pull back slightly and fold in the edges. Roll tightly and seal. Be careful to ensure all the air is removed.

Heat oil in a large wok on medium heat and deep-fry until golden brown. Drain and serve.

You can vary the filling considerably, to suit your personal taste and preference. For a healthier option, steam the spring rolls or, why not, opt for fresh spring rolls. Soak rice paper in warm water until soft, use fresh ingredients such as herbs, lettuce, cucumber, tuna, salmon, etc. Roll and... serve!

This is a perfect appetizer which can be made well in advance. This recipe uses rice paper, but you can also use spring roll pastry. Look for it in the freezer section of your Asian supermarket. Seal it with egg white.

A break in the Isaan

Pi Toon is a great friend of mine and she has always been an unbelievable source of inspiration. It was she who introduced me to Pa Sida's restaurant, as she used to work in that neighbourhood. This time however she is not in Bangkok as she is teaching a diving course in the south. When we do manage to get together we talk for hours about food and delicious dishes, and those hours just talking about food are always the greatest of pleasures. She has guided me countless times through the Thai culinary world and has taught me a huge amount about her culture. Today, Tuk, a really great guy, is my street food guide. I first got to know Tuk, when he was working with his very good friend Ploy at the Taewez guest house. Ten years on and he has grown into a man, and just as so many Thai people, he has a warm heart and a nose for good food.

If you are looking for a culinary treat, then you should go to the boat stop at Tha Wang Lang and visit Pa Sida's (auntie Sida's) restaurant. This spirited lady has been running her thriving business here, for fifty years. Proudly she shows us a photo of the Thai king when he came to eat at her restaurant. This is a mecca for lovers of the specialities from the Isaan, the North East region of Thailand. Auntie Sida sits, surrounded by a plethora of pestle and mortars, preparing the most fantastic **green papaya salads** (*som tam*). Meanwhile the restaurant is filling up with students, hospital personnel and other regular market goers. They all come to satisfy their midday hunger with sticky rice (*khao niaw*) and **grilled chicken** (*gai yang*), **warm salads with minced meat** (*laab*) or **grilled beef salad** (*nua naam tok*) and of course her famous green papaya salad of which there are at least eleven different varieties on the menu; everything from the standard version with peanuts (*som tam thai*) to slightly more exotic varieties with salted black land crabs (*som tam poo*) or with fermented fish (*som tam pa laa*). As for me, today I order a **bamboo shoot salad** (*sub nor mai*).

Tuk jokingly calls us 'the Belgiamese' and he introduces me to a papaya salad flavoured with a special kind of water insect. Wow! The refined, fragrant, and may layers of flavour this insect imparts to the dish makes my taste buds tingle. I order *tab waan*, a salad with cooked liver that is similar to *naam tok nuea* but is prepared with liver instead of grilled beef. It is served with sticky rice and you eat it with your hands, by bringing together a small ball of the sticky rice with your fingers and using it to scoop up the food or to mop up the sauce.

Khun Tuk tells me how he and Ploy used to buy a bag of sticky rice and grilled chicken liver skewers. They would put the chicken liver into the rice and squash them together. It is a wonderful, tasty and fatty comfort food.

Green papaya salad

ส้มตำ

som tam

The nickname for this dish, *pok pok* is an onomatopoeia; alluding to the sound made by the wooden pestle in the mortar. So give it a try; ask for either som tam or pok pok when ordering, and you will be served the same fantastic dish.

Ingredients

200 g green papaya
1-2 garlic cloves
2-5 small chilli peppers
1 pinch of salt
1-2 tsp. palm sugar
2 snake beans, cut in 1 cm lengths
2 tbsp. roasted peanuts
4 cherry tomatoes, halved
2 tbsp. dried baby shrimps
1 apple aubergine, sliced (optional)
2-3 tbsp. fish sauce
1-2 tbsp. lime juice

Peel and shred the green papaya. Pound the garlic with chillies, salt, and sugar in a clay mortar with a wooden pestle. Add snake beans, peanuts, tomatoes, dried shrimps and if using, the apple aubergine. Keep pounding and mixing simultaneously with a large spoon.

Season it with fish sauce and lime. Fold in the green papaya and continue pounding and mixing until the papaya is coated with the dressing.

This is a basic recipe and as you can tell from auntie Sida's extensive menu there are a lot of variations possible. You can substitute the green papaya with cucumber (*tam taeng*) or add grated carrot.

Som tam with sticky rice and grilled chicken (*gai yang*) is a match made in heaven!

The 'som tam' vendor is the easiest of all to recognise. When you see a clay or wooden mortar and wooden pestle, you can be absolutely sure they are making 'som tam'. Originally a dish from the north-east, the poorer and sometimes regarded as inferior Isaan-region, it is hugely popular, especially among women (no fat, good for digestion), and has spread nationwide. Whatever the reason for its popularity, it is a fabulous, fresh and tangy delight. We just can't get enough of it!

A terracotta or wooden pestle and mortar is chosen to prepare this dish, because unlike the granite mortar used for making a curry paste for example, in this case you don't want to grind the ingredients too finely, but just press out the juices. Use a long handled spoon to mix the ingredients together well.

Don't be surprised if the som tam seller asks you how many chillies you would like. You decide how hot you want it and the dish will be prepared to suit your own taste. I have personally witnessed customers ordering ten chillies in their green papaya salad, and with a completely straight face.

If the som tam seller says *phet mai khrap/ka*, then he is asking if you would like it hot. If you are not a fan of spicy, answer with *mai phet khrap/ka*. If you want a medium hot dish then ask for *phet nitnoi khrap/ka*, and if you are feeling adventurous go full out for the *phet phet khrap/ka*.

Grilled chicken
ไก่ย่าง
gai yang

The best version of *gai yang* that we ate was in the market in Mukdahaen, a border city in the Isaan by the Mekong River.

Ingredients

1 small chicken
3 coriander roots, scraped and chopped
10 white peppercorns
3 garlic cloves
¼ tsp. salt
1 stalk of lemongrass, hard bottom end cut off; outer leaves removed, white part finely chopped
½ tbsp. turmeric (optional)
1 tbsp. fish sauce
1 tbsp. sugar
wooden sticks and iron wire (optional)

Cut chicken in half along the breastbone. Flatten out (butterfly), wash and dry.

Take a pestle and mortar, pound coriander root, white peppercorns, lemongrass, garlic and salt into a fine paste. When you're using turmeric, add it at this point. Add fish sauce and sugar. Vigorously rub this paste into chicken, outside and inside. Marinate for 4 hours in the refrigerator. Fix the marinated chicken between wooden sticks and secure with iron wire if using. This will make it easier to turn the chicken. Chargrill chicken for about 20 minutes until cooked, turning regularly.

Serve with sticky rice, sweet chilli sauce and a selection of raw vegetables.

If you don't want to use a whole chicken, you can prepare this recipe with drumsticks, chicken wings or chicken breast.

Thai shallots are smaller and more refined in taste than ours.
If you can not find them, you can use the ones from your supermarket.

:○: — **Boiling**
ต้ม

Warm, minced chicken salad
ลาบไก่

laab gai

This is an amazing hot and sour salad, bursting with flavours but low in fat.

Ingredients

1 skinless chicken breast
1 pinch of salt
4 tbsp. water or chicken stock
2 tsp. galangal, chopped
1 shallot, sliced finely
1 spring onion, sliced in rings
1 tsp. chilli powder
5 tbsp. lime juice
3 tbsp. fish sauce
1 tbsp. sticky rice, toasted and ground
1 handful coriander leaves
1 handful mint leaves

Take a sharp knife or cleaver and mince chicken finely with salt. Bring water to the boil, add galangal and cook the meat until done. There should be a little liquid left, if too much, discard the excess.

Turn off the heat and add shallot, spring onion, chilli powder, lime juice and fish sauce. Check seasoning. It should taste hot and sour and then salty.

Just before serving, add the toasted rice powder and finish with the fresh herbs.

This dish should be eaten with sticky rice (*khao niaw*) and a selection of raw vegetables such as snake beans, white cabbage, Thai basil and cucumber. Eat it with your hands: form a ball of sticky rice, dip it in the *laab* or use this rice ball to scoop up some of the *laab*.

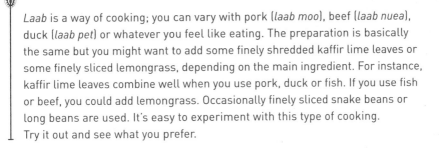

Laab is a way of cooking; you can vary with pork (*laab moo*), beef (*laab nuea*), duck (*laab pet*) or whatever you feel like eating. The preparation is basically the same but you might want to add some finely shredded kaffir lime leaves or some finely sliced lemongrass, depending on the main ingredient. For instance, kaffir lime leaves combine well when you use pork, duck or fish. If you use fish or beef, you could add lemongrass. Occasionally finely sliced snake beans or long beans are used. It's easy to experiment with this type of cooking. Try it out and see what you prefer.

:◊: — *Grilling*
ยาง

Grilled beef salad from Isaan
น้ำตก เนื้อ

naam tok nuea

'Naam tok' literally means waterfall, referring to the meat juices that forms on top of the meat as it grills. The nutty taste of toasted rice powder combined with the charcoal flavour of the meat is to die for!

Ingredients

3 tbsp. lime juice
2-3 tbsp. fish sauce
1 pinch of sugar
1 tsp. chilli powder
150 g beef (tenderloin)
2 shallots, sliced finely lengthwise
1 spring onion, sliced finely in rings
1 stalk of lemongrass, hard bottom end cut off; outer leaves removed, white part sliced very finely in rings (optional)
1 handful of mint leaves
toasted sticky rice, ground to a powder in a mortar

First make the dressing by mixing the lime juice with fish sauce, sugar and chilli powder. Balance well; this dressing should taste spicy, sour and salty.

Grill the meat, preferably on a wood charcoal grill for that authentic flavour, to your taste. Cut beef in slices (bite-size). Don't waste the meat juices, save as much as you can.

Combine beef and juices with shallot, spring onion, lemongrass (when using), and fresh herbs. Finish with dressing and toasted rice powder.

For an extraordinary experience, try this at home with fresh tuna steak!

Actually, *naam tok* is related to *laab*. The difference being that the meat is sliced and grilled instead of minced and boiled. Serve it the same way you would serve *laab*: with sticky rice and a selection of raw vegetables such as snake beans, white cabbage, Thai basil and cucumber. In Thailand this is usually prepared with beef, although sometimes pork is used.

— **Boiling**
ต้ม

Bamboo shoot salad
ซุปหน่อไม้

sub nor mai

Ingredients

1 handful bamboo shoots,
julienned finely
1 spring onion, chopped
1 shallot, sliced
1 tsp. chilli powder
3 tbsp. lime juice
1 tbsp. fish sauce
1 tbsp. toasted sticky rice,
ground finely
1 handful mint and
coriander leaves

Bring a little water to the boil.
Boil the bamboo shoots for approx-
imately 1 minute, discard most of
the water.
Turn off the heat. Add spring onion,
shallot and chilli powder.
Season it with lime juice, fish sauce
and finish with toasted rice, mint
and coriander.

Don't buy canned bamboo shoots
for this recipe. Use fresh ones. Ask
for them in your Thai supermarket.

Rediscovering Chinatown

I have arranged to meet a talented and passionate Thai guide, Benz. She works for a company called Taste of Thailand Tours (www.tasteofthailandfoodtours.org) who organise culinary excursions around Bangkok. This is a great new addition to the range of activities on offer for tourists and astute tour operators are happy to jump on the band wagon.

Willingly I hand over the reins to Benz, and she leads me through the Sam Yan market and along part of the busy Rama IV road. In the evenings the footpath between the underground station at Sam Yan and the Hualumphong train station is magically transformed into a culinary festival site. We pull up a chair and dig into a bowl of **egg noodles with crab, choy sum and wonton dumplings** (*ba mee kaew pu*). Benz is not particularly hungry at the moment so while I eat she tells me how she would love to study to be a chef, as she is equally as passionate about cooking as she is about talking about food. We saunter on, past Hualumphong and end up in Chinatown. Benz like many of her fellow countrymen has a sweet tooth, and she tells me about the **pumpkin with custard** (*sang khaya phak tong*) she makes at home. We stop at a well-known spot where they are serving **coconut with green jelly beans** (chendol), she orders two portions and we are served the sweet desert with green chendol strips in plastic beakers to take away, while Benz and I swap notes on favourite dishes and the best places to get them.

The year of the goat is approaching and Chinatown is preparing for the Chinese New Year; young and old alike are busy hanging up garlands of lanterns. Chinatown is a wonderful and unusual place and Benz introduces me to this world full of mystique and well-kept cooking secrets. It is a bustling place, busy with trading and doing business, serving authentic recipes that have been passed down through generations. On the corner a Chinese man stands with his modest cart, he proudly tells us that has been selling **stewed pork on rice** (*khao kha moo*) on this same street corner for 30 years. Mopeds come and go with people ordering a serving to take away. The secret of his khao kha moo, and what makes the meat a soft as butter, is that the pork stews for almost six hours.

I ask if Benz knows of a good place to get the peppery soup of **rolled noodles with pork** (*kuay chap*) and she takes me to a corner restaurant, where they mince the pork belly and cook the pork offal. A little further on Benz orders some kanom tuay, a steamed **coconut baked custard** a little sweet treat to take home. As I say good bye to my wonderful companion on this fantastically educational and inspiring evening, I wholeheartedly hope that with all her passion she achieves her dream of one day becoming a chef.

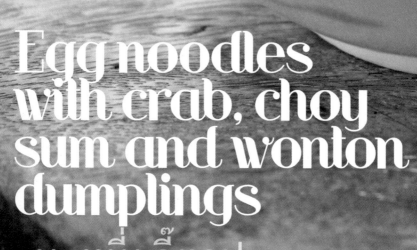

Egg noodles with crab, choy sum and wonton dumplings

 บะหมี่เกี๊ยวปู

ba mee kaew pu

morning **afternoon evening** *night*

— Boiling — Steaming
ต้ม   นึ่ง

Ingredients

100 g crab, flesh only
4 choy sum leaves
300 g dried egg noodles,
cooked for 3 minutes in water
100 g roasted red pork
(moo deng - see p. 145), sliced

Sauce

2 tsp. sesame oil
3 tbsp. oyster sauce
2 tbsp. light soy sauce
2 tbsp. dark soy sauce
2 shiitake mushrooms, sliced
120 ml water
1 tbsp. flour mixed with 2 tbsp. water
(optional)
½ tsp. ground white pepper
pinch of salt
½ tsp. sugar

Wontons

200 g minced pork
2 garlic cloves, finely chopped
1 cm ginger, finely chopped
1 tbsp. oyster sauce
1 tbsp. light soy sauce
½ tsp. ground white pepper
½ tsp. salt
20 wonton skins
1 egg, lightly beaten

First make the wonton parcels. Combine the minced pork, garlic and ginger thoroughly and season well with the oyster sauce, light soy sauce, pepper and salt. Take a wonton skin and place a teaspoon full of the minced pork mixture in the middle. Brush the edges of the wonton skin with a little beaten egg and seal the edges together. Create a nice shape by giving the top edges of the wonton parcel a little twist. Repeat the process with the remaining wonton skins and filling mixture.

Now make the sauce. Put the sesame oil with the oyster sauce, light soy sauce and dark soy sauce, into a pan over a medium heat. Add the shiitake mushrooms and water. If desired thicken the sauce by adding the flour and water mixture. Season to taste with the pepper, salt and sugar. Remove the pan from the heat and set aside.

Cook the filled wonton parcels in a pan with water. This will only take a few minutes. Drain and set aside.

In a steaming basket, steam the crab meat. This will only take 1 or 2 minutes to cook through.

In a pan of boiling water quickly blanch the choy sum. Drain and set aside.

Reheat the noodles in boiling water, drain well and divide between the serving plates. Pour some sauce over each serving of noodles and garnish with the choy sum, wonton parcels, crab meat and the sliced red pork.

morning **afternoon evening** *night*

◊ — **Steaming**
นึ่ง

Pumpkin with custard
สังขยาฟักทอง

sang khaya phak tong

Sang khaya is slang for 'dirty' in Thai, it refers to the brown filling inside this tasteful dessert.

Ingredients

1 small Japanese
pumpkin
8 eggs,
lightly beaten
16 tbsp. coconut cream
8 tbsp. palm sugar
1 pinch of salt
4 pandan leaves,
shredded

Wash and dry the pumpkin.
Take a sharp knife, cut off the top of the pumpkin so you form a kind of lid.
Scoop out all the seeds.
Mix the eggs with the coconut cream, palm sugar and salt. Whisk until the sugar has dissolved. Add the shredded pandan leaves.
Pour this mixture in the pumpkin through a sieve.
Steam the pumpkin for about 30-40 minutes, depending on the size of your pumpkin.
Leave to cool at room temperature and divide into parts.

:◊: — **Boiling**
ต้ม

Coconut with green chendol jelly beans

ลอดช่องสิงคโปร์

lod chung Singapore

Whether you are in Singapore, Penang or Bangkok, you can find this sweet and refreshing snack sold on every street.

Ingredients

230 g green chendol strips, lod chong

125 g palm sugar

1 tbsp. sugar

180 ml water

crushed ice

750 ml thick coconut milk, sweetened to taste with 4 tbsp. sugar

Rinse the green chendol strips under cold water. Allow to drain and keep to one side.

Put the sugars into a pan and add the warm water when the sugar is beginning to melt. You should end up with a nice thick sauce, but still with a pourable consistency. Keep to one side.

Divide the crushed ice into bowls. Add 2 tablespoons of the green chendol strips and 2 tablespoons of the sugar syrup. Finally, pour 4 tablespoons of the sweetened coconut milk over each portion.

:◊: — **Boiling**
ต้ม

Stewed pork on rice

ข้าวขาหมู

khao kha moo

We know: it looks rather unappetizing at first but do try it. The meat is utterly succulent and the five-spice powder gives it an astonishing aroma.

Pork

2 tsp. black peppercorns
1 tsp. salt
6 garlic cloves, chopped
4 coriander roots, scraped and chopped
2 tbsp. vegetable oil
4 tbsp. palm sugar
1 tbsp. water
1 kg pork leg, shaved and cleaned
enough water to cover
1 tsp. dark soy sauce
4 tbsp. soy sauce
1 nutmeg
3 cloves
3 star anise
4 cm cinnamon stick
½ tsp. five spice powder
4 eggs, hardboiled, peeled

Sauce

2 medium chillies
1 coriander root, scraped and chopped very finely
2 garlic cloves, chopped finely
½ tsp. salt
2 tbsp. vinegar

Pound the peppercorns with salt in a mortar, until the peppercorns are completely pulverised. Add coriander root and garlic whilst pounding. The result should be a smooth, fragrant paste. In a large pan, heat the oil on medium heat. Fry the paste until all the aromas are released. Add the palm sugar and lower the heat. The sugar has to melt, not burn. Stir, add 1 tbsp. of water and keep stirring. Prick the pork leg a few times with a fork and add it to the pan, making sure it is completely covered with the sauce.

If the pan is not big enough, transfer everything to a large pot, add water so that everything is covered. Turn the heat to medium. Add the soy sauces, nutmeg, cloves, star anise, cinnamon, five spice powder and eggs. Cover with a lid and bring to the boil. When boiling, remove the lid and skim off the foam. Keep simmering on a low heat for 2-3 hours until the meat is tender. Stir regularly.

In the meantime, pound the chillies, coriander root, garlic and salt in a mortar. Stir in the vinegar and set aside. Cut the pork in bite-sized strips and serve on a bed of rice. Quarter the eggs and put some of them next to it. Serve with the green vegetables and a small bowl of sauce.

Serve with steamed or stir-fried greens (e.g. Chinese broccoli, spinach, pak choi) and cooked rice

There are many fiercely kept secrets regarding this dish, each street food vendor improving and perfecting the recipe and often handing it down only to the next generation. Every portion comes with a serving of raw garlic and small chillies, and taking a little of this on the spoon with each mouthful will help cut through the fat. Thai people are generally fond of fat, and it is often considered to be the best bit of the meat. If they want to please you, they will make sure you get a fair portion of it, but if you are not so keen, you can say kho mai sai man ka/krap. 'I don't want the fat, please'.

Rolled noodles with pork

+ กวยจั๊บน้ำใส

kuay chap nam sai

These wide flat rice noodles, which curl up into tubes when cooked, remind me of the Italian pasta, penne.

Ingredients

½ tsp. finely chopped coriander root
½ tsp. finely chopped fresh ginger
1 tsp. white peppercorns
¼ tsp. coarse sea salt
2 garlic cloves, roughly chopped
1 tbsp. vegetable oil
1 l pork stock
1 star anise, toasted
1 tsp. coriander seeds, toasted
½ tsp. cumin seeds, toasted
1 clove, toasted
1 cinnamon stick, toasted
½ tsp. Chinese five spice powder
2 tbsp. light soy sauce
1 tbsp. dark soy sauce
1 tsp. sugar
200 g wide, kuay chap noodles
100 g crispy pork belly cut into blocks, 1 cm wide and 3 cm long (moo khrob see p. 146)
2 spring onions cut into rings
1 handful coriander leaves
½ tsp. fried garlic
½ tsp. ground white pepper

In a mortar grind the coriander root, ginger, white peppercorns, salt and garlic to form a smooth paste. Over a low heat warm the oil in a large pan and fry the paste for 1 minute.

Add the pork stock and bring to the boil. Place the toasted star anise, coriander seeds, cumin seeds, clove and cinnamon stick into a spice bag, add to the stock and allow to infuse as the stock continues to cook, but for no longer than 15 minutes. Season the stock, with the five spice powder, light and dark soy sauces and the sugar.

Cook the kuay chap noodles in water. Drain the noodles and divide onto the serving plates. Portion the pork belly and divide over the noodles, then pour some of the pork stock over each. Finish off with the spring onions, coriander, fried garlic and white pepper.

Kuay chap noodles are often served with pork offal, such as lung, intestines, liver or tripe. Though perhaps a little less adventurous, this recipe using crispy roasted pork belly (moo khrob) is just as delicious.

There are also different versions of the stock: a light clear variety (nam sai) as above or the darker (nam kon) version, where the pork or offal is first seared, resulting in a dark brown coloured stock.

Thai coconut baked custard

ขนมถ้วยตะไล

khanom tuay

This desert is available in different versions. The white variety when only coconut is used, the green has the addition of pandan, or as a combination of green and white layers.

Ingredients

60 g rice flour
20 g tapioca flour
200 ml coconut milk
150 g sugar
1 tsp. pandan extract

Combine the two flours together. Gradually add the coconut milk while continuously stirring. Mix in the sugar and pandan extract. Allow the batter to stand for 30 minutes.

Divide the batter into ramequins, this will make about enough for 10. Place into a steamer and over a gentle heat steam the pots for about 10 minutes.

Serve with a sweet caramel sauce. You can make a caramel sauce by carefully melting 75g of sugar in a heavy bottomed pan, then add 100ml of hot water and continue to warm gently over a low heat for about 15 minutes until the sauce turns golden brown in colour.

Modern Bangkok

Second only to flying, travelling by train, is by far the most relaxed and safest form of transport for long distances in Thailand. Just beyond north west Chinatown you find the pretty art deco station Hualamphong, standing in stark contrast to the adjacent spotless, modern metro. Bangkok is a city of extremes, the incongruities adding to the magic and atmosphere of this international city. You can dine on the 64th floor of a sky scraper (The Dome) which will set you back 4000 baht, and then a few hours later you could be enjoying equally delicious food, sitting on a plastic chair in a dark alleyway, for a mere 20 baht.

I have always had a certain fascination for train and bus stations and airports, for their bustling energy and continuous state of change, with people in constant motion, on their way to a new destination or just back from some adventure or another. Strategically placed along this tide of humanity you will often find stalls selling snacks that are easy to eat on the go: **deep-fried banana** (*kluay thod*), **Thai fishcakes** (*thod man pla*), **grilled fermented sausages** (*sai krok*) or grilled banana (*kluay ping*).

I get a motorbike taxi to take me to the Victory Monument. From here you can take one of the many mini-buses going to the North of Thailand, but today I am heading for the skytrain (BTS) which will quickly get me to the centre of modern Bangkok. Around the monument and in the surrounding side streets there is a huge amount of street food on offer, which the commuters make use of, to eat while they are waiting. As it is lunch time I head to the north east corner of the monument where for 10 baht I pick up some **noodle soup with beef** (*kuaytiaw nuea*). A friendly woman is standing close to the stairs the leading to the entrance of the skytrain, selling **grilled sticky rice in banana leaf** (*khao niaw ping*). Smiling she asks me if I want to try some, and free of charge she hands me the little package, freshly grilled and still warm.

morning **afternoon evening** night

— **Deep-Frying**
ทอด

Deep-fried banana

กล้วยทอด

kluay thod

This filling snack is sold at virtually every train- and bus station. Often deep-fried pumpkin is on offer too.

Ingredients

6 small sweet bananas
200 g rice flour
200 g flour
1 tsp. bicarbonate of soda
200 ml water
100 ml coconut milk
½ tsp. salt
50 g sesame seeds
3 tbsp. sugar
50 g coconut pulp
oil for deep-frying

Peel the bananas and cut length-wise in 4. Mix flour with the other ingredients. Dip the bananas into batter and deep-fry until golden.

Steamed fishcake
หอหมกปลา

ha mok pla

This is an impressive way to serve steamed fishcake.

Fishcake

1 big banana leaf, heated on a flame or blanched to make it soft and flexible
15 Thai basil leaves
175 g white fish fillet, chopped very finely
2 tbsp. red curry paste
2 tbsp. thick coconut cream
3 kaffir lime leaves, shredded finely
1 tbsp. fish sauce
1 egg, lightly beaten

For garnish

1 large red chilli, deseeded and finely sliced in strips
1 kaffir lime leave, shredded very finely
extra Thai basil leaves
2 tbsp. thick coconut cream

First, make the 4 banana leaf cups. For each cup cut out 2 squares of 12,5 cm x 12,5 cm. Use a glass or a bowl with a diameter of 10 cm, as a template to cut out 2 circles. Place the circles mat sides together; make sure the leaf fibres are forming a cross. Make 4 equidistant pleats, 1 cm wide x 4 cm long, (working 'north' then 'south', 'east' then 'west') pointing towards the center of the circle, fastening with a staple or a wooden tooth pick as you go. The result should be a square-shaped cup. Put some basil leaves at the bottom and set aside.

Put the fish in a mixing bowl, add curry paste, coconut cream, kaffir lime leaves and fish sauce. Combine well and mix in the beaten egg. Divide this mixture into the cups, making sure they are no more than 2/3 full.

Steam the cups for 20 minutes until cooked, garnish with chilli, kaffir lime leave, basil and a little coconut cream and serve immediately.

☼ — *Grilling*
ยาง

Grilled fermented sausages
ไส้กรอก
sai krok

Ingredients

Ingredients

500 g minced pork
100 g sticky rice (optional)
5 coriander roots, chopped
6 garlic cloves, chopped
1 tbsp. salt
1 tbsp. fish sauce
1 tbsp. sugar
sausage skins
young ginger, diced
chilli, sliced in rings
roasted peanuts
iceberg lettuce

- Steam the sticky rice for 20 minutes until cooked. Leave to cool.
- Pound the coriander roots, garlic and salt in a mortar into a smooth paste. Add sticky rice and pork and season with fish sauce and sugar. Fill the sausage skins with this mixture, make about 7 cm long sausages, making a knot to finish each sausage.
- Grill over charcoal for about 7 minutes until cooked, turning regularly.
- Cut in pieces and serve with some diced ginger, a (small) piece of chilli, some peanuts and some iceberg lettuce.

It's sometimes available in a fermented version. After preparations, they leave the sausages for a few days. Most foreigners are not used to this somewhat sour taste. In Thailand they use a grill shaped like the roof of a house (like a pyramid), so the fat can drip down.

:Ö: — **Boiling**

ต้ม

Noodle soup with beef
+ กวยเตี๋ยวเนื้อ

kuaytiaw naam nuea

Noodle soups are always available and are eaten at any time of the day. If however you only want the noodles without the soup, then ask for *kuaytiaw haeng*.

Stock

1 kg beef bones
1 beef shank
1 pinch of salt
1 pinch of sugar
enough water to cover
12 crushed black peppercorns
2 tbsp. dark soy sauce
1 cinnamon stick
2 coriander roots, scraped and bruised
1 handful of coriander stalks
1 star anise
3 garlic cloves
1 knob of galangal, sliced
1 stalk of lemongrass, bruised
2 stalks of Chinese celery, chopped roughly
1 onion, quartered

Beef balls

100 g minced lean beef
1 large pinch of salt
1 large pinch of ground white pepper

Fried garlic

6 garlic cloves, chopped
60 ml peanut oil

Bowl

200 g dried rice noodles, soaked in warm water for 30 minutes
50 g rump of beef, sliced very finely
1 handful of soy bean sprouts
1 spring onion, chopped to garnish
coriander leaves to garnish

Put all the ingredients for the stock into a large pot, bring to the boil, turn the heat down low, cover and simmer for 3-4 hours, skimming regularly. Take out the shank, remove the meat from the shank and slice finely. Strain the stock and put the meat from the shank back in. If you have time and want to remove all excess fat, leave the stock to cool in the refrigerator. The fat will harden on top of the stock and can easily be removed.

Combine the beef, salt and pepper, form into small balls and set aside. Fry the garlic in the oil until golden and set aside. Bring the stock back to the boil. Meanwhile bring another large pot of water to the boil and blanch the meatballs, soy bean sprouts and noodles one small portion at a time.

A handy utensil to do this is a wire-mesh ladle as you can easily 'fish out' the ingredients from the water. You can either put the raw slices of beef in your bowl or briefly blanch them in the water. Place noodles, soy bean sprouts and slices of beef in a bowl, add a few meatballs, some meat from the shank, and pour over the hot stock. Garnish with the spring onion, coriander leaves and top with the fried garlic oil.

There are two types of commonly used noodles: rice noodles and egg noodles. Egg noodles are easy to recognise because of their yellow colour; rice noodles are white. Most noodles come in various sizes. In Thailand, rice noodles come in three sizes, usually all three available at a food stall. 'Sen yai' are wide noodles, 'sen lek' are thin noodles and 'sen mii' are very thin noodles, or rice vermicelli.

When Thai people say that a person is 'sen yai', it means that he or she is a VIP, Very Important Person.

Like many dishes in Thai cuisine, noodles can be prepared in endless variations. You can use chicken or vegetable stock, sometimes even duck broth. You can use ingredients such as fish balls, roasted red pork, wontons, chicken breast, etc.

🜄 — *Grilling*
ย่าง

Grilled sticky rice in banana leaf

ข้าวเหนียวปิ้ง

khao niaw ping

Fillings can be banana, taro, mung beans, black beans or shredded coconut. If you don't like surprises, point and ask for it *sai arai khrap/ka*, literally 'with what'.

Ingredients

1 large banana leaf
200 g sticky rice, soaked in cold water overnight or at least 3 hours in warm water
wooden or bamboo skewers, soaked in water for at least 30 minutes

Hold the banana leaf over an open flame. This makes it supple and gives the leaf a beautiful dark green colour. Alternatively, the banana leaf can be blanched briefly in order to get the same result. Cut the leaf into rectangles (10 cm x 5 cm).
Put 2 rectangles in a T-shape, top piece underneath. Steam the sticky rice for about 15 minutes until cooked. Leave to cool. Divide in small portions.
Place a portion on the top piece of banana leaf. Fold in the edges and roll tightly. Secure with a skewer.
Grill over charcoal for 6 minutes, turning regularly.

Nowadays banana leaves are not so popular to wrap up food. This is one of the few dishes where it has not lost its packaging function. Maybe it's because of the delicious flavour the banana leaf infuses during grilling. Often eaten as a bite on the go or carried as a type of lunch snack.

105

On the skytrain

This afternoon I have an appointment to meet up with my old street food buddy Yves, so I buy a BTS ticket from the machine and go a few stops in a northerly direction till I reach the staggering Chatuchak weekend market. I have arranged to meet up with Yves, who lived in Hanoi for many years, and with whom I have traversed many a street food city on several continents, at the Oto Kor market. It is here you will find the highest quality ingredients, and is the place where the high echelons of society come to stock up on first class fruit and vegetables. We celebrate our reunion with a light snack of **leaf-wrapped bits** (*miang kam*), a perfect warm up for our taste buds.

Together we jump back on the BTS-skytrain to Chitlom, where we are meeting another Thai friend Khun Tripathi. Socially committed Khun Tripathi works as a journalist for, amongst others, The Nation, an important English language Thai newspaper. Our destination is Sukhumvit soi 38. After five in the afternoon the road undergoes a metamorphosis, changing into an atmospheric street food happening and everything is being set up in readiness for the evening. **Grilled fish in salt** (*pla pao*) is being prepared over a charcoal fire, while the man at the stall opposite puts the final touches on his phat thai, a stir-fried noodle dish with scampi. Daniel Thangier, famed for his gourmet hamburgers, is setting up white plastic tables next to his food truck. It is a modern street food truck which looks just as if it has been plucked off the streets of New York, and a happy mix of expats and Thai people are served by the friendly staff. It is just the beginning, and the woks and grills here will be working late into the night.

With concern for the people who work on the food stalls, Khun Tripathi tells me about the industrialization of street food in Thailand. There are an increasing number of food stalls selling factory prepared and deep frozen food. So not everything is as fresh as you may think and not every street food vendor prepares everything himself. He also tells me of the exploitation of immigrant workers in the fish and street food industries. Happily though I also hear how many simple folk are able to survive and make a living thanks to the street food industry and they are proud when people enjoy the food they have made; a feeling that I am sure many cooks can relate to.

Back on the BTS we change at SIAM BTS station and travel in the direction of Saphan Taksin. We have been invited to meet Tom Vitayakul, connoisseur and patron of Thai arts, who runs a gourmet restaurant in Ruan Aroi in the Silom district. The restaurant is housed in a traditional wooden Thai building, of the type which is today becoming a rarity. This is Bangkok through and through: a traditional building rubbing shoulders with a modern sky scraper in the red light district. Tom gives me a lot of interesting tips and after a good long chat Yves and I set off again to continue our culinary expedition. Before embarking on the next leg of our journey though, to the atmospheric Convent Road, we stop for a rest and of course something to eat at the Lumphini Park where we order some **stir-fried crab with yellow curry**. It is a bit of a trek to Convent Road, but well worth the effort as this is where we are going to eat **braised goose**

in brown gravy (*harn pra loh*) I had never eaten goose before, and it is extremely tender and delicate in taste. After another short skytrain ride we get off at the Saphan Taksin Bridge to continue our day's culinary orgy and we saunter on with full bellies to the Charoeng Krung.

Close to the spice shop on the Charoeng Krung you can find a jewel of a Muslim restaurant, which I usually visit for the Indian roti and a portion of the **oxtail soup** (*soup hang wua*). However today we walk into the street opposite the Robinson Shopping Complex for some **stir-fried noodles with pork and gravy** (*raat na*). How much is it possible to eat in one day?

Meanwhile Yves brings me up-to-date with the latest culinary newcomers and trends in the city. He tells me about the modern food truck scene, the farmers' and organic markets that have recently become very hip, and about the neighbourhood he moved to a few months ago, Ari. Living close to a skytrain or underground station is a definite advantage these days in Bangkok, as despite intensive efforts the traffic is an outright disaster. Getting hungry again we hop back on the skytrain and head for Ari, a fantastic, atmospheric neighbourhood with food stalls set up everywhere, which especially during the week, is buzzing. Yves insists on taking me for a night cap on Summer Street, another new street food concept that has been set up by a few enthusiastic entrepreneurs. Utilising a section of a car park, with nothing more than a few tarpaulins stretched to keep off the rain, local street food chefs grill the freshest seafood over charcoal-fuelled table top fires. Yves also gets me to try a few of the locally brewed beers; local breweries, a cool street food concept with an international feel; this is *über hip Asian style*!

Yves and his girlfriend Tracey offer me a bed for the night, so the next day, out of curiosity and for the freebies we visit one of the organic markets in the Thong Lo district an up market neighbourhood known for its countless Japanese restaurants. I am surprised by the international character of this 'green market' and it makes me happy to see how many people here are genuinely interested and engaging with organic food. This market could certainly hold its own in comparison to other food concepts in New York or London. Welcome to modern Bangkok!

:◊: — **Mixed**

Leaf-wrapped bits
เมี่ยงคำ

miang kam

Miang kam is a prime example of Thai cuisine, a perfect balance of different flavours all combined into one.

Paste

4 slices galangal, toasted
1 large pinch of salt
2 small chillies
½ tsp. shrimp paste, toasted
1 tbsp. dried baby shrimp, ground
3 tbsp. grated coconut, toasted
1 tbsp. peanuts, roasted and ground

Sauce

5 tbsp. palm sugar
75 ml water
4 tbsp. fish sauce
3 tbsp. tamarind water

For garnish

16 betel leaves (*bai champluu*) or young spinach leaves
1 tbsp. diced lime
2 tbsp. grated coconut, toasted
2 tbsp. roasted peanuts
1 tbsp. diced young ginger
2 tbsp. dried baby shrimps, toasted
2 tbsp. diced shallots
1-3 small chillis, finely sliced in rings

For the paste, pound the ingredients together in a mortar, adding them one by one, until smooth.

For the sauce, heat the sugar with water. When the sugar is dissolved, let simmer for several minutes until it thickens. Add fish sauce, then stir in the paste and continue to simmer for a few minutes. You should be able to smell the galangal. Add the tamarind water and turn the heat down. Keep simmering for a few more minutes. Remove from the heat. Leave to cool.

How to serve: Put the leaves in the middle of a plate and arrange little piles of the lime, coconut, peanuts, ginger, shrimp, shallot and chilli around them. Every guest can take a leaf, fold it like a small envelope, filling it with the ingredients according to personal taste, top it with some sauce, close it and eat it in one bite. It is important that you don't bite it in half but put the whole thing in your mouth. This is to ensure that you experience the layers of flavor in one go.

Variations: Add pomelo, fresh oysters or mussels to the array of filling ingredients.

You can find this snack pre-packed on the streets of Bangkok, usually with all the ingredients packed separately in small plastic bags.

— *Grilling*
ยาง

Grilled fish in salt
ปลาเผา

pla pao

Amazingly simple, less is more.

Ingredients

1 sea bass

4 stalks of lemongrass

250 g coarse sea salt

First clean the fish (scale, gut and wash), pat dry. Cut off the hard bottom end of the lemongrass, bruise with a knife to release all the flavour. Stick the stalks of lemongrass through the fish via its mouth, this makes a kind of herbal skewer. Cover both sides with salt. Grill over charcoal for about 15 to 20 minutes, turning regularly until cooked.

The spicy seafood dip (*naam jim thaleh*, see p. 206) goes well with this. Lemongrass is a superb stuffing for fish, it adds a distinctive freshness.

◊: — *Stir-Frying*
ผัด

Stir-fried crab with yellow curry

ปูผัดผงกะหรี่

poo phat pong kari

Pak chee roi na is a well known Thai saying that means 'to top it with coriander'. It's used for cover-ups or when things are made to look better than they are.

Ingredients

250 g fresh crab meat
2 tbsp. vegetable oil
1 onion, sliced in rings
1 garlic clove, chopped
1 egg, beaten
2 tbsp. yellow curry powder
2 tbsp. soy sauce
1 tbsp. fish sauce
¼ tsp. sugar
2 stalks of Chinese celery, chopped roughly
1 handful of coriander leaves

Put a wok on medium to high heat. When warm, add oil, onion and garlic and stir-fry for a few seconds. Add beaten egg and stir-fry till the egg is cooked. Add curry powder and crab and stir-fry until crab is cooked. Add soy sauce, fish sauce and sugar. Combine well. Add Chinese celery, stir and finish with fresh coriander leaves.

Braised goose in a brown gravy
ห่านพะโล้
harn pra loh

Chinese in origin, braised goose or duck is a dish usually simply served on a bed of rice.

Ingredients

1 goose 3 kg
3 tbsp. vegetable oil for frying
2 garlic cloves, crushed
1 l chicken stock
750 ml dark soy sauce
250 ml light soy sauce
250 ml Shaoxing rice wine
50 g sugar
¼ tsp. salt
5 star anise petals
2 cinnamon sticks
1 tbsp. fennel seeds
½ tsp. ground cumin
coriander leaves to garnish

Cut the goose in half. Put 2 tablespoons of the oil in a large pan and warm over a medium high heat. Fry each half separately in the pan until they are nicely browned, then remove from the pan and keep to one side.

Add another tablespoon of oil to the pan and fry off the garlic for 2 minutes. Next pour in the chicken stock and bring to the boil. Add the soy sauces, the Shaoxing rice wine, sugar and spices and bring back to the boil. Place the goose halves back in the pan and if necessary add some water, enough to cover the meat. Allow to simmer for two hours on a low heat or until the meat is tender.

Take the goose out of the sauce and remove the meat from the bone and cut into thin slices. Arrange the meat on a plate and pour over the sauce. Garnish with a few coriander leaves and serve with rice and a chilli-vinegar dipping sauce.

For this dish you can easily substitute duck if you can't get goose.

🔥 — **Boiling**
ต้ม

Oxtail soup
ซุป เนื้อวัว

soup hang wua

Oxtail is a forgotten cut of meat, but oh so full of flavour! The dried spices used in the recipe give a clue to the Arabic origins of this dish.

Ingredients

2 tbsp. vegetable oil
1.2 kg oxtail, 5 to 6 pieces, most of the fat removed
1.5 l water or enough to cover the oxtail
½ tsp. cumin seeds
1 tsp. coriander seeds
1 cinnamon stick
1 tsp. fennel seeds
4 green cardamom pods
1 tsp. turmeric powder
1 tsp. ginger powder
1 tsp. ground white pepper
1 tsp. chilli powder
½ tsp. salt
1 onion, chopped into half rings
2 medium potatoes, chopped into 2cm cubes
4 tomatoes, chopped
2 spring onions, in rings
1 handful coriander leaves
1 tbsp. fried onions
lime juice, to taste

Put the oil in a large heavy pan, and warm over a medium high heat. Brown the oxtail off on all sides. Add the water and gently bring to the boil. Turn the heat down and allow to simmer for at least one hour. Put the cumin seeds, coriander seeds, fennel seeds and cardamom pods into a spice bag and place into the pan and allow to infuse in the cooking liquid but for no longer than 15 minutes. Season the soup with the remaining dried spices. Add the chopped onion and potatoes to the pot and cook for 10 minutes. Then add the tomatoes and continue cooking for a further 10 minutes.
Serve out into bowls and garnish with the spring onion, coriander leaves, fried onion, and lime juice. Serve with rice.

Stir-fried noodles with pork and gravy
กวยเตี๋ยวราดหน้าใส่หมู
kuaytiaw raat na sai moo

Ingredients
4 tbsp. vegetable oil
1 handful wide rice noodles,
soaked and drained
2 tbsp. sweet soy sauce
2 garlic cloves, chopped
100 g pork, cut in strips
1 stalk of Chinese broccoli,
cut diagonally
8 tbsp. chicken stock or water
1 tsp. yellow bean paste
2 tbsp. dark soy sauce
1 tbsp. light soy sauce
1 tbsp. tapioca flour

Heat 2 tablespoons of oil in a wok on a medium heat and stir-fry the noodles with the sweet soy sauce for 2 minutes. Set aside.

Heat the remaining oil on a low heat and fry garlic until golden. Turn up the heat and add pork.

Keep stirring until the pork changes colour. Add Chinese broccoli whilst stirring. Add stock or water, yellow bean paste, soy sauces. Stir in the tapioca flour and let the sauce thicken, like gravy. Add the noodles and combine well.

Sam Phraeng

This seemingly sleepy area is an oasis of calm and feels like it is a million miles away from the hectic city, as if time has stood still. Traditional restaurants, some that have been here for fifty years, are housed in old Chinese shops and quietly go about their business. The quality is high, and fittingly so, in the illustrious shadow of the princely palaces. Sam Phraeng covers three streets respectively named after the former princes (Phraeng Nara, Phraeng Phuton, Phraeng Salpasart).

For years Chote Chitr has been a favourite haunt for food lovers, and I often drop in on this part of town for a visit. For traditional Thai cuisine this is the place to be. The café is in a quiet and pleasant neighbourhood, on a side street just off the Tanao Road. As a rule I order the **crispy noodles** (*mee khrob*), which are served with the sour fruit, som sa, and the **banana flower and chicken salad** (*yam hua pli*). Scrumptious!

More than ninety years ago, Khun Chote, a doctor in traditional Thai medicine, opened the Chote Chitr as a medicinal herb shop. His wife, who formerly worked in the kitchens of the palace, began preparing and serving meals, using the healing herbs and spices in the ingredients. Until very recently they were still serving the incredibly healthy **vegetable soup** (*gaeng liang*), bursting with vegetables and herbs and generously seasoned with black pepper. This highly nutritious soup, according to my good friend Pi Toon, was traditionally, though not exclusively, eaten by breastfeeding mothers. Recent studies by the institute of nutrition at the Mahidol University in Bangkok, showed that eating gaeng liang can help in the prevention of colon cancer, and more studies are being undertaken to further investigate the health benefits.

You can imagine how disappointed I was when I found myself standing in front of closed doors on my last visit. So I rang on the bell, only to discover they are now only open for a couple of days a week, there is uncertainty as to who will take the business over and the future of the restaurant is still not secure.

Kao Niaw Korpanich, on the corner of the Tanao Road is the place to be for **sweet sticky rice with coconut and mango**, where they have been selling this fantastic dish for 75 years. Their secret is simple: use only the best ingredients and prepare it with love.

You know you are in the right place when you see the mango sellers stalls in front of the shop, with a huge variety of mangoes on offer. The most expensive is the oak wrong mango, sweet and juicy, or there are also dokmai, less juicy and slightly firmer but always sweet, and tong dam that tastes slightly sourer.

Also on the Tanao Road and equally well known is the Khanom Buang Phraeng Nara. This small and unpretentious concern is on the right-hand side as you walk from Ratchadamnoen Avenue, where the owner patiently makes **crispy coconut pancakes with salty or sweet topping** (*khanom buang*). Though he used to work on the Thai railways he has now become a fervent khanom buang-maker, and not only for the locals as he also exports his sophisticated snack abroad, even far beyond Asia. While I curiously snoop around the Sam Phraeng district looking for some interesting new places, I see a monk sitting under a parasol spooning in ice-cream. It was in a similar way that I came across an old house where **coconut sorbet** (*sherbet mapraw*) and **mango ice-cream** (*eye krim* *mamouang*) were on the menu. The ancient wall mounted ventilator blew out a sultry breeze; while one of the clients assured me that this was the best ice-cream in all Bangkok, so good in fact he travelled here, sometimes three times a week, just to get some. Slightly further up the street is a business that has been around forever cooking and selling various sorts of **red pork** (*moo deng*) and **crispy pork** (*moo khrob*). Roasted pork on a bed of rice with brown gravy is a not to be missed classic.

Next, I come across a man skilfully cooking noodles with a pair of long chopsticks. But this is really something for the culinary adventurous, noodle soup with pig's brains. Personally, I am not crazy about entrails.

Well represented in Bangkok, I like to describe khao gaeng restaurants, as street food buffets, where you have a choice of a wide assortment of freshly prepared and freshly cooked dishes. My favourite rice dish is **stir-fried rice with shrimp paste** (*kao klut kapi*) the strong taste of the shrimp paste does not overpower the dish, but gives a depth and body to the flavour. I head to lunch at one of my favourite khao keng restaurants on the other side of the district with a view over the royal palace and the military academy. The friendly owner comes to explain what each dish contains. But as we have arrived quite a bit after midday she hasn't got too much left in stock. 'This evening all fresh dishes' she calls out in a friendly way. As side dishes I order some **deep-fried chicken** (*gai tod*) and **Thai mackerel in sweet sauce** (*pla tuu priao wan*). I love this area for its quiet and slow tempo, so I round off the day reading, sitting in the coffee shop on the corner of Thanon Tanao, the tranquil atmosphere bringing back happy memories of my earlier visits here.

New to the area and extremely handy for the visitor, are the descriptive boards that now hang in every traditional restaurant. This makes street food exceptionally accessible and offers a journey back through history. Also new and almost unique in Bangkok are the *bike lanes* which run along the Tanao Road. This is a clear sign that in Bangkok too, they are busy with alternative and green options for the transport infrastructure.

:◊: — **Deep-Frying**
ทอด

Crispy noodles
หมี่กรอบ

mee khrob

There are a countless number of recipes for these deep-fried rice noodles, covered with a thick, sweet dressing.

Noodles	Soak the noodles in water for 10 minutes, drain
100 g dried thin rice noodles	and coat with beaten egg. Leave to dry for at least
1 egg, lightly beaten	2 hours or preferably overnight.
1 handful of soybean sprouts	Pound the coriander root together with the garlic,
1 big, red chilli, in julienne	white peppercorns and salt until smooth. Fry this
1 handful of Chinese chives,	paste on a low heat in oil until golden, add yellow
chopped	bean paste and sugar. Once the sugar is dissolved,
1 handful of coriander leaves	add the eggs. Keep stirring. Simmer until thick,
oil for deep-frying	and then add lime and orange juice. Simmer for
1 tbsp. orange zest, grated	a few more seconds and take off the heat.
	Leave to cool.
Sauce	Heat the oil on medium to high heat.
2 coriander roots,	Deep-fry the noodles in a few batches.
scraped and chopped	The noodles will puff up and change colour,
4 garlic cloves	stir and remove with a wire ladle.
10 white peppercorns	Drain on a paper towel. Reheat the sauce carefully
1 pinch of salt	on a low heat, add the crispy noodles. Make sure
2 tbsp. vegetable oil	the noodles are evenly coated with the sauce.
200 ml yellow bean paste	Gently mix with the soybean sprouts, chilli,
200 g sugar	Chinese chives and grated orange zest.
2 eggs, lightly beaten	
100 ml lime juice	
3 tbsp. orange juice	

In Thailand a fruit, called 'som sa' is used instead of the orange.
It tastes slightly more bittersweet, but orange or tangerine can be
used as substitutes.

Chinese chives are a member of the onion family, but the flavour is more like garlic. They can be substituted with a mix of normal chives and chopped garlic.

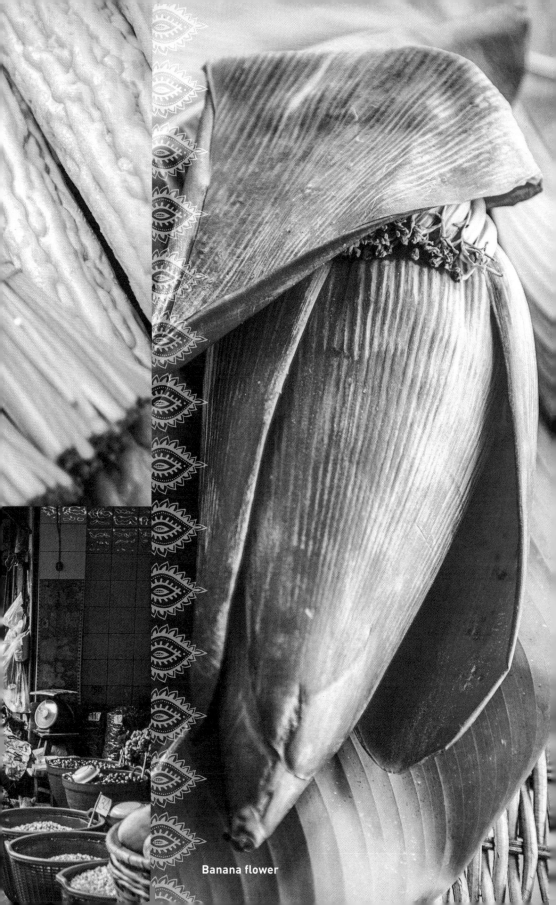
Banana flower

Banana flower and chicken salad
ยำหัวปลี

yam hua pli

Ingredients

1 banana flower

1 tbsp. lime juice

water

200 g chicken breast

200 ml coconut cream

1 tbsp. roasted chilli paste

1 tbsp. fish sauce

1 tsp. sugar

3 tbsp. lime juice

1 stalk of lemon grass, white part sliced finely

deep-fried cashew nuts (optional)

1 handful of coriander leaves

2 kaffir lime leaves, shredded very finely

2 small red chillies, deep-fried

Remove the outer leaves of the banana flower. Quarter lengthwise and remove the core. Slice very finely and leave to soak for at least an hour in a mixture of water and lime juice to reduce the bitter flavour.

Boil the chicken in the coconut cream for about 10 minutes on a low heat until cooked.

Remove the chicken but keep the coconut cream to make the dressing. Cut chicken into fine slices.

Mix the coconut cream with chilli paste, fish sauce, sugar and lime juice. Combine the drained banana flower, lemon grass, cashew nuts, if using and chicken and incorporate all this with the dressing. Garnish with the coriander, kaffir lime leaves and chilli.

Select only firm and fresh looking banana flowers. They are also known as 'banana blossom' and 'banana heart'. If you can't find them in your Asian supermarket, you can substitute it with Belgian endives.

Vegetable soup
แกงเลียง
gaeng liang

Most of the herbs and vegetables are hard, if not impossible to get your hands on outside of Asia so we suggest some alternatives.

Paste

1 tsp. black peppercorns
4 tbsp. finger root or krachai, chopped
1 tbsp. garlic cloves, chopped
4 tbsp. shallot, chopped
4 small chillies, chopped
12 tbsp. oyster or straw mushrooms, chopped
1 and ½ tbsp. salted bean paste

Soup

1 l water or chicken stock or vegetable stock
1 pinch of salt
8 tbsp. Thai or Japanese pumpkin, cut in bite-sized pieces
16 tbsp. of young bottle gourd or 1 small cucumber, cut in bite-sized pieces
16 tbsp. of angle loofah or 1 small courgette, cut in bite-sized pieces
12 prawns, shelled and deveined (optional)
1 tsp. light soy sauce
1 pinch of palm sugar
1 handful of ivy gourd or young spinach
1 handful of lemon basil

Pound the ingredients for the paste gradually in a mortar using a pestle until smooth. Bring water or stock and salt to the boil and add paste. Stir well. Add pumpkin, gourd or cucumber, angle loofah or courgette and simmer until soft. When using prawns, this is the time to add them. Add soy sauce and palm sugar and mix. Add ivy gourd or young spinach and lemon basil and serve immediately.

Finger root is named for its hand and finger-like appearance. It's also known as 'lesser ginger' and 'lesser galangal'. Besides the use in herbal medicine, finger root is commonly used in Thai cooking. It has a sharp and spicy flavour and is beneficial in the digestion process. If you can't find fresh finger root, look for it in the freezer section of your Asian supermarket.

Liang means 'at hand' or 'grown nearby' referring to the fresh ingredients used in this curry-like soup.

Sweet sticky rice with coconut and mango

ข้าวเหนียวมะม่วง

khao niaw mamuang

A must-try! This combination is awesome. Use Thai mangos, irreplaceable in this recipe.

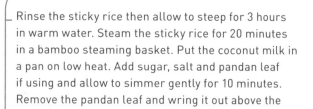

Ingredients

400 g sticky rice
water for steaming
400 ml coconut milk
125 g sugar
1 tsp. salt
1 pandan leaf (optional)
1 or 2 ripe mangos
toasted sesame seeds
(optional)

Rinse the sticky rice then allow to steep for 3 hours in warm water. Steam the sticky rice for 20 minutes in a bamboo steaming basket. Put the coconut milk in a pan on low heat. Add sugar, salt and pandan leaf if using and allow to simmer gently for 10 minutes. Remove the pandan leaf and wring it out above the coconut milk.

Pour half of this mixture over the warm sticky rice. The sticky rice has to be moist but not drowning in coconut milk. Leave to stand for 15 minutes.

Peel the mango and cut in small cubes. Put the sticky rice in small serving bowls, spoon over a few tablespoons of the remaining (warm) coconut mixture and scoop some mango cubes on top. Sprinkle with some sesame seeds. The perfect afternoon snack before heading towards the Grand Palace and Wat Po!

It is said that 'people from the Isaan stick together like sticky rice'. In the poorer Isaan region people have to rely on each other much more just to get through life.

Pandan leaves are used in Thai cooking for their distinctive flavour but also in the Thai bathroom to add a scent to the water used for washing. You could say it's the vanilla of Thailand. You may even notice the aroma of pandan in cars or taxis. Also known for its medicinal qualities, it keeps the heart and liver in good condition, relieves fever and soothes a sore throat.

Because sticky rice uses less water to grow than other types of rice, they chose to cultivate this variety in the arid northeast region of Thailand. This is why in the northeast and to some extent in the north sticky rice is a mealtime staple. Boiling sticky rice is not a good idea: the rice grains disintegrate and all you are left with is a thick pulp. When it is steamed the sticky rice becomes a translucent white, whereas normal rice becomes an opaque white.

A 'khanom buang' maker is a skilled worker; it takes a refined technique and perfect timing to form the crispy pancakes. They come in two varieties. The sweet yellow one with golden threads (*foi tong*) and the savoury orange one made with shrimp and coriander. These pancakes should be very crispy. Don't be tempted by the inferior whipped cream version that you can find at most food markets.

— Frying

Crispy coconut pancakes with salty or sweet topping

ขนม เบื้อง

khanom buang

This is a great example of the Portuguese influence on the Thai desert repertoire. This can be seen in the use of eggs and the half-moon shape.

Dough

500 ml water
4 tbsp. cocoa powder (e.g. Ovaltine, Milo)
500 g toasted yellow bean powder
1 kg rice flour
6 eggs
700 g sugar

Filling

15 eggs, only the egg white
2 kg coconut palmsugar
>>

For the dough, mix the cocoa powder with water. Add yellow bean powder and rice flour. Knead until dough doesn't stick. Mix in eggs thoroughly. Add sugar and knead until the sugar has dissolved completely.

For the filling
Take a clean, grease-free bowl. Put your mixer on medium-high speed and mix the egg whites until you see soft peaks. Gradually add the coconut palmsugar and keep mixing until sugar has dissolved and the egg whites are forming stiff peaks.

For the savoury topping
Pound the coriander root with the peppercorns, using a pestle and mortar, until smooth. Heat water and sugar in a large pan over medium heat, stir in the paste. Add prawns, salt, fresh coconut and food colouring. Stir until the water has evaporated. Set aside. >>

Savoury

5 coriander roots,
scraped and chopped

50 g white peppercorns

500 ml water

24 tbsp. sugar

300 g fresh prawns, minced

1 tsp. salt

3 fresh coconuts, flesh shredded

red or orange food colouring

Sweet

golden threads

For garnish

shredded fresh coconut

toasted sesame seeds

fresh coriander leaves

For a savoury 'khanom buang'

Put a skillet on medium heat. Carefully spread a thin layer, forming a little pancake. Cover with a thin layer of the filling. Dab some of the savoury topping on it and garnish with shredded coconut, sesame seeds and coriander leaves. Fold the pancake in half while removing it with a spatula.

For a sweet 'khanom buang'

Put a skillet on medium heat. Carefully spread a thin layer, forming a little pancake. Cover with a thin layer of the filling. Dab some of the sweet topping on it and garnish with shredded coconut and sesame seeds. Fold the pancake in half while removing it with a spatula.

As you can see this is not a simple recipe. There is a Thai saying that literally translated means: 'you can't make khanom buang with your mouth' meaning to say that 'if you don't know what you are doing perhaps it is better to leave it alone'.

Coconut sorbet

เชอร์เบท มะพร้าว

sherbet mapraw

Ingredients

400 ml coconut milk
100 g sugar
200 g grated fresh coconut
¼ tsp. salt

Warm the coconut milk in a pan and add the sugar. When the sugar has completely dissolved add in the salt and the grated coconut. Put the sorbet in the freezer, either divided into individual portions or in one large freezer-proof container.

If you are using an ice cream maker, follow the instructions on the machine.

Mango ice cream

ไอศครีม มะม่วง

eye krim mamouang

Never too cold for ice cream in Thailand.

Ingredients

2 large, sweet mangos
4 egg whites
100 g sugar
220 ml double cream

Peel the mangos, and remove the flesh. Finley chop the mango then puree in a food processor. With a food mixer beat the egg whites until they are light and fluffy and forming soft peaks and continue beating as you add the sugar. Mix the cream and mango puree together then fold in the beaten egg white mixture. Divide into portions and place in the freezer.

If you are using an ice cream maker, follow the instructions on the machine.

NUTTAPORN
COCONUT ICE CREAM
ナタポン アイスクリーム

:○: — *Grilling*
ยาง

Grilled red pork
หมูแดง

moo deng

In every Chinatown in the world, you will see this red pork on offer.
Originally Chinese, you can tell by the use of five-spice powder,
this delicacy has found a firm place in the Thai kitchen.

Ingredients	Method
1 pork tenderloin	First make the marinade. Mix all the ingredients except for the pork. Marinate the pork in this mixture for at least 3 hours in the refrigerator.
1 tbsp. fish sauce	
1 tbsp. dark soy sauce	Remove from the marinade and sear the pork on all sides over a charcoal grill.
1 tbsp. sugar	
1 tbsp. fresh ginger, chopped	Turn regularly and baste with leftover marinade until cooked (about 15 minutes).
½ tbsp. sesame oil	
½ tsp. red food colouring	Leave to cool. Cut into very thin slices.
1 tsp. five-spice powder	

Grilled red pork is often used in noodle soups or served on a bed
of rice. You can easily spot where it is being served as you will see
the red pork hanging from a hook.

Crispy pork
หมูกรอบ

moo khrob

This is truly authentic Thai food, very easy to make but a little
time-consuming. Start preparations well in advance.

Ingredients

3 tbsp. light soy sauce
1 pinch of salt
1 pinch of sugar
1 kg pork belly, washed
5 tbsp. salt
3 tbsp. vinegar
oil for deep-frying

Mix soy sauce with a pinch of salt and sugar
and marinate the pork belly in the refrigerator
for 2 days.

Remove from the marinade and steam the pork
belly for 30 minutes until cooked. Cool but do not
refrigerate. Make lengthwise incisions, about ½ cm
deep, being careful, to only cut through the skin,
not the meat. Prick the meat with a fork; generously
rub it in with salt and vinegar.

Leave it to dry at least 1 night, preferably 48 hours.

Brush off dried salt and deep-fry until pork skin has
bubbled and crackled. Drain well, cool and cut in
slices.

Crispy pork is used in several dishes, like noodle soups, stir-fries,
but is also extraordinary in *yam*. It adds a fantastic, salty, crispy flavour.
It's easy to tell if a food stall has crispy pork: it usually hangs on display.

🔥 — **Stir-Frying**
ผัด

Stir-fried rice with shrimp paste
ข้าวคลุกกะปิ
khao kluk kapi

If you have some leftover cooked rice,
this lunch dish is the perfect way to use it up.

Ingredients

½ tbsp. finely chopped
coriander root

1 garlic clove roughly chopped

¼ tsp. coarse sea salt

2 tbsp. vegetable oil

1 tbsp. shrimp paste toasted
for a few minutes in
aluminium foil in a pan

300 g cooked rice

1 tbsp. rice vinegar

1 tsp. sugar

In a pestle and mortar grind the coriander root, garlic and salt to form a smooth paste.

Put the vegetable oil into a wok and warm over medium high heat. Add the coriander root paste and stir-fry for a minute or so, until the aromas are released. Add the shrimp paste and continue to stir-fry until well blended and evenly distributed.

Add the rice and continue to stir-fry carefully making sure that the rice does not stick or burn. Season to taste, with the rice vinegar and sugar.

Serve with simple garnishes and/or side dishes; for example julienne of green mango, fried egg, dried prawns or as shown here fried chicken (gai tod - see p. 150)

If possible you should use rice that was cooked the day before as it will be slightly drier and therefore less likely to clump together during stir-frying.

◌ — **Deep-Frying**
ทอด

Deep-fried chicken
ไก่ทอด

gai thod

Sprinkle, Soi Polo-style, some deep-fried garlic on top.

Ingredients

4 garlic cloves, chopped

4 coriander roots, chopped

10 white peppercorns

4 tbsp. flour

1 egg, lightly beaten

2 tbsp. water

2 tbsp. fish sauce

2 tbsp. light soy sauce

8 chicken legs or drumsticks

oil for deep-frying

sweet chilli dip

for serving (see p. 206)

Pound the garlic, coriander root and white peppercorns in a mortar until smooth.

Mix the paste with the flour, beaten egg, water, fish sauce and soy sauce.

Dip chicken in batter and deep-fry until golden and crisp.

Serve with sweet chilli sauce.

🔥 — **Stir-Frying**
ผัด

Thai mackerel in sweet sauce
ปลาทูเปรี้ยวหวาน

pla tuu priao wan

I was introduced to this popular little fish by my good friend Pi Toon.

Ingredients

2 tbsp. vegetable oil
2 Thai mackerel or 4 mackerel fillets
4 bird's eye chillies, in fine rings
4 garlic cloves, finely chopped
2 tbsp. fish sauce
2 tbsp. sugar
4 tbsp. tamarind juice
(1 tbsp. tamarind paste squeezed out into 4 tbsp. water)
100 ml water
1 handful coriander leaves

Warm a wok over medium heat, and add 1 tablespoon of the vegetable oil. Fry the fish for two minutes on each side until golden brown then take the fish out of the wok and keep to one side.

Add the remaining tablespoon of oil to the wok and fry the chilli and garlic for 1 minute.

Add in the fish sauce, sugar and tamarind juice. Return the fish to the wok and pour in the water. Allow the fish to absorb some of the liquid.

Garnish with the coriander leaves and serve with rice.

In Thai street food Thai mackerel is so prevalent you just can't ignore it. You can eat it simply steamed, with a classic dipping sauce (*nam phrik kapi* – p. 207) or even in a salad with chilli and lemon grass (*yam pla tuu*).

The national dish

Despite the wide range and variety of food on offer, the average tourist in Thailand, will often limit himself to just a few dishes. Phat thai (and rightly so) will usually be one of them. If you want a taste of phat thai in its most refined form, then this is the place to be. I return to visit Thip Samai, next to the Wat Saket temple in the north of the city. From five o'clock in the afternoon the line starts to build, people politely joining the line that winds past the fire spewing woks to wait for their **stir-fried noodles** (*phat thai*). I am on my own today and as I take my seat to wait for my phat thai it makes me feel a little bit lonely. The pleasure of eating is surely something to be shared with friends, and as I sadly look around I know that is something everyone else in the restaurant knows too.

Possibly the best and most hygienic phat thai business in the city, Thip Samai opened its doors in 1966, and can thank its continued success, and loyal clientele on its consistent care to use only the best ingredients. To avoid the rainy season in the Maha Chai district, Mrs. Samai moved to a house in Bangkok where she could open a restaurant. She asks three times as much as the average phat thai seller, but it is worth every extra baht. There are many variations on offer, such as phat thai wrapped in an omelette or phat thai with green mango and crab. The dishes are always served with banana flowers, soya bean shoots and spring onion, and can be seasoned to your own taste with chilli, fish sauce and grilled peanuts.

Historically the preparation of phat thai goes back to the time of Ayutthaya when Vietnamese traders introduced noodles to Thailand. The original name 'kway teow pad' also gives away their Chinese origin. In power from 1938 to 1944 the nationalist Prime Minister Phibun, who was in power from 1938 to 1944 changed the name of the country from Siam to Thailand. His government also promoted the use of rice noodles and the cultivation and export of rice and therefore also influenced the consciousness of the people of Thailand. And not without success, today phat thai is according to CNN in the top four of the most popular dishes in the world.

ผัดไท

焼き鵄とっても美味しいですよ!あなたもとりこになります♨

PADTHAI

Accompaniments

1 handful of soy bean sprouts

a few sprigs of Chinese chives, chopped in 5 cm lengths

¼ small banana flower, cut into strips, soaked in water with some lime juice

1 lime, cut in wedges

4 tbsp. roasted peanuts, ground roughly

extra sugar

extra chilli powder

:🔥: — **Stir-Frying**
ผัด

Stir-fried noodles with prawns
ผัดไทย

phad thai

In fact, this is derived from a Chinese dish but with a few Thai modifications (adding tamarind water for instance) and is regarded as a very Thai dish. Phat thai became popular during the war in Vietnam, when a lot of American soldiers came to Thailand for R&R. That's why some food vendors started to add ketchup to it. Luckily that variation didn't last very long.

Ingredients

4 tbsp. fish sauce
2 tbsp. palm sugar
2 tbsp. white sugar
2 tbsp. tamarind water
250 g thin dried rice noodles, soaked for 1-2 hours in water
3 tbsp. vegetable oil
2 shallots, chopped finely
2 garlic cloves, chopped finely
3 tbsp. dried baby shrimps
1 egg, lightly beaten
4 tbsp. firm tofu, deep-fried and diced in small cubes
2 tbsp. pickled radish, chopped
1 tsp. chilli powder
1 small bunch of Chinese chives, chopped into 2 cm lengths
1 handful of soy bean sprouts

Simmer the fish sauce, palm sugar, white sugar and tamarind water until sugar is dissolved. Set aside.

Drain noodles.

Heat the oil in a wok over medium heat and gradually fry the shallots, garlic and dried shrimps. Add egg, turn heat down low and keep stirring. Add tofu and white radish, and then add the noodles. Turn up the heat and make sure that the noodles are evenly coated. Mix in the prepared sauce and the chilli powder whilst stirring. Add the Chinese chives and the bean sprouts.

Put on a plate and serve with accompaniments.

Thai cooking techniques

The abundance of food can seem overwhelming and confusing for someone visiting Thailand for the first time. But with a little patience you can navigate your way through this culinary maze.

First and foremost it is good to remember each food seller specialises in one sort of food. They all more or less keep to their own category, due to the specific equipment needed to prepare the dish. The food stalls are not fully equipped professional kitchens; they only have what is absolutely necessary.

By looking at what type of equipment is being used on the stall; or if you like the 'hardware', you can determine the type of food being served. Next you need to see which ingredients, or 'software', are on offer, and these will often be on display either in a glass cabinet or a bamboo basket.

Once you have got the hang of recognising the utensils (hardware) and the ingredients (software) it becomes child's play to identify the dish being made. The hardware is what determines the method of cooking.

Grilling (yang)

Comparable to a barbecue, and just a popular, this type of food stall is a common sight on the streets of Bangkok. Traditionally coal is used for the archetypal smoky flavour it gives to the food. Sometimes the food is laid directly onto the grill, but for more delicate ingredients such as fish, a sort of protective wrapping is used. Banana, coconut or pandan leaves are generally preferred to aluminium foil. Not only does it look more attractive, but the leaves help to keep the moisture in, they have a natural anti-stick layer, and they also infuse a hint of their flavour into the food. But remember to be careful and don't eat the packaging!

Some food sellers will have a small terracotta pot containing the glowing coals with a grill over the top, on which your food will be cooked to order. Others have a larger grill, a bit like our western style barbecues, where the food is on display while cooking. Grilling over charcoal adds an extra flavour dimension to the dishes, and one of the classics, **grilled dried squid** (*pla muek yang*) is often sold from a bicycle which the seller moves around balancing their charcoal fire on top.

Boiling (tom)

If you come to a stall and see a gas fire and an aluminium cooking pot then you need to look at the ingredients on show. The main categories you will find are (noodle) soups, stews, and finely chopped warm salads (laab). Some sellers will have a wide variety, others just one dish, but you can almost always customise your meal to suit your personal taste, by for example choosing the type of noodle or the type of meat used. It is also often possible to ask for extra ingredients to be added, just show them what you want. With a noodle dish you first have to choose the sort of noodle you want, 'mi', for egg noodles, 'sen lek' for thin rice noodles, 'sen yai', for thicker rice noodles. Then you let them know if you want to eat your noodles dry, 'heng' or with soup, 'naam'.

Steaming (neung)

Steaming is often preferred to boiling as a cooking method. Because the ingredients are cooked in the steam coming off a boiling liquid and do not come into direct contact with the liquid itself, the flavours and textures of the food are better preserved. It is an extremely healthy way of cooking, but it goes without saying you get the best results with the freshest of ingredients.

The typical Thai steamer has several layers, is usually made out of aluminium, and comes in a range of sizes. The bottom pan holds the liquid, and you can use one or more layers, which are stacked on top of each other and they hold the ingredients to be cooked. The food that needs the longest cooking time is placed in the lowest layer and the whole thing is covered with a lid so that the steam does not escape.

Thai cooks don't only use the steamer to cook food but also to keep it warm, as is the case for the classic Chinese steamed buns (*salapao*) and steamed fishcakes in banana leaves (*ha mok pla*). For smaller snacks, such as the Thai dim sum (*khanom jeep*), food sellers opt for smaller steamers made of bamboo. These also have several different layers but the bottom section is different, and is placed above a cooking pot filled with boiling liquid. In many of the food markets you will also find steamed mackerel (*pla tuu*) presented in these small bamboo steaming baskets.

There is also a beehive shaped type of steaming basket, which is used for cooking and serving sticky rice in. Water is brought to a boil in an aluminium cooking pot; the basket containing the rice is placed inside then covered with a lid or a towel to prevent steam from escaping.

Frying

The 'hardware' for frying is very easily recognisable and pretty much everywhere. We have split this section into three categories: Deep frying, the griddle, and stir-frying.

Deep-Frying (thod)

Despite the fact that they deep-fry a lot, Thai cuisine still enjoys a reputation for being very healthy. This is because usually only one ingredient or a small part of the meal is cooked in this way, to give a crunchy element to a dish. In any case the portions are smaller and most Thai people will compensate when eating fatty foods by also eating vegetables and/or fruit: yin and yang.

Thai deep-frying is done using a large wok, often with a handle on each side, and heated over a hot gas burner. The size of the flame is important, because if the oil cools down too quickly as ingredients are added, the food absorbs too much fat. On the other hand if the oil is hot enough the moisture will be sealed into the food and as the trapped moisture turns into steam and escapes from the cooking food, it prevents the oil from going in. The food is lifted in and out of the hot oil using a large Chinese skimming spoon. On a food stall selling deep fired food you will always see a rack on which cooked food is rested to let as much oil as possible drain off, keeping it crispy.

The griddle (phat)

This is actually a bit of an in-between category, half way between grilling and frying. The food is quickly fried on a special flat griddle plate or in a specially designed mould, (for example the coconut puddings). Phad thai are often cooked on the griddle and so too **mussel pancakes** (hoi thod). Most commonly nowadays chefs use a gas flame to heat the griddle pan, but sometimes you will spot a hardcore traditionalist popping up with a coal fire.

Stir-Frying (phat)

Stir-frying in a wok is perhaps what most people would think of, as associated with Thai cuisine, but most Thai dishes don't necessarily need to be cooked in a wok. Sometimes it is true, only a wok will do, but most of the time it is just used because it is handy. For example to prepare a small portion of soup, or as a pan to use with a steaming basket there are no hard and fast rules regarding the necessary hardware. However it is essential to use a wok for stir-fried dishes. Another of my favourite dishes is **stir-fried water spinach** (*pak bung fai deng*). The preparation for this dish is what takes the longest, as all the ingredients have to be carefully washed and cut into bite-size pieces beforehand. After that is done though it is very fast: heat the wok over a high flame, add the oil and let it get nice and hot, then in go the ingredients, added in the right order. Then simply a quick stir-fry till everything is cooked through and you are done! Because of the high temperature and the finely chopped ingredients the whole process only takes a couple of minutes. Stir-frying is a really quick and healthy way of cooking, preserving the maximum amount of flavour and nutritional value of the food. The unique shape of the wok means that the bottom section gets the hottest, with the sides remaining slightly cooler, so you can move cooked food to the side while continuing to cook in the hot bottom part. And of course you can't stir-fry without a spatula to stir the food. If you see a food stall with a wok over a flame, you have to look at the ingredients on display to be able to decide which dish is being sold.

Mixed

The ingredients for some dishes are (finely) ground together, whereas others are simply mixed and added to another dish as a dressing. If you see a food stall displaying a large wooden or terracotta mortar, then you can guarantee they are selling the renowned green papaya salad. Another typical piece of hardware is a mixing bowl. Again you need to take a look at the ingredients on display in the glass case, or on ice to decide what this food seller has to offer.

'Yam' is a spicy-sour salad with any number of interchangeable ingredients, but nearly always served with a dressing made of fish sauce, lime juice, sugar, chilli, and a mix of fresh herbs. If you are health conscious and counting the calories, you will certainly have noticed that the list of ingredients does not include any fat, the total opposite of a vinaigrette dressing. Yam pla muk or spicy squid salad is another one of my favourites. Important to remember: in Thailand a 'yam' is generally very hot and spicy!

— *Grilling*
ยาง

Grilled dried squid
ปลาหมึกย่าง

pla muek yang

Listen for that unique tune and if you are lucky to spot one,
order a portion, and enjoy it while you still can.

Ingredients

1 fresh medium-sized squid,
cleaned

250 g salt

- Rub in the squid vigorously with the salt and leave to dry in the sun or at least 2 hours in an oven (100°C).
- Flatten the squid in a press. Alternatively you can use a pasta machine.
- Grill the squid over charcoal, about 3 minutes each side.

Once ordered, you get your serving in a piece of newspaper, folded
into a bag, together with a sweet chilli dip and/or a sweet dip with
peanuts. The sweetness balances the saltiness extraordinarily well.

🔥 — **Frying**

Mussel pancakes
หอยทอด
hoi thod

Try this after a night of drinking to alleviate your hangover the day after.

Ingredients

500 g mussels,
scrubbed and shelled
2 tbsp. vegetable oil
1 egg, lightly beaten
1 handful of soy bean sprouts
1 spring onion, chopped
1 tbsp. light soy sauce
1 tbsp. fish sauce
1 tsp. sugar
1 handful of coriander leaves
1 pinch of white pepper

Batter

3 tbsp. rice flour
3 tbsp. flour
1 pinch of salt
1 egg
200 ml water

Begin by thoroughly mixing all the batter ingredients together. Add the mussels and set aside. Heat the oil in a skillet or a wide flat pan and ladle in the batter to make a pancake. When the pancake begins to look crusty around the edges, flip it to cook the other side.
Break up the pancake and fry the egg in between. Add soy bean sprouts and spring onion and stir well. Add soy sauce, fish sauce and sugar to season and garnish with the coriander leaves and pepper.

Serve with sweet chilli sauce.

:◊: — *Stir-Frying*
ผัด

Stir-fried water spinach or morning glory
ผัดผักบุ้งไฟแดง

phat pak bung fai deng

Phat fai deng literally means: 'cooked with red fire' and you will sometimes see this dish being prepared with spectacular theatricality. To get the wok to the searing hot temperature required, occasionally the flames go inside the wok itself, also giving the water spinach a smoky flavour. Some street chefs go a step further tossing the vegetables into the air as the flame enters the pan, skilfully catching everything as it falls back down. A bit dangerous if you ask me; and I strongly advise that you don't try this at home.

Ingredients

250 g water spinach
1 tbsp. vegetable oil
2 garlic cloves, crushed
1 red medium chilli, sliced finely
2 tbsp. yellow bean sauce
1 tsp. sugar
2 tbsp. light soy sauce
6 tbsp. water or chicken stock

Put the water spinach in iced water, this will keep the water spinach nice and crisp to stir-fry. Drain. Heat the wok, add the oil and stir-fry garlic, chilli and yellow bean sauce on medium heat. Add the water spinach; turn the heat up high and stir-fry until the leaves soften. Reduce the heat and add sugar, soy sauce and water or chicken stock. Serve immediately.

The Chinese influence

Perhaps one of the biggest influences on Thai cuisine has come from the Chinese. Even before the city of Bangkok existed there were Chinese immigrants living in the area. Where the royal palace now stands was a Chinese neighbourhood, but when construction of the palace began residents were forced out and moved to Yawalat. During the day it is lovely to wander through the narrow alleyways around Yawalat, and Chinatown is a world of its own – a city within a city – with different temples, another language and different food on offer.

Available from Hong Kong to Singapore and perfectly demonstrating just how influential the Chinese were, is the dish **chicken on rice** (*khao man gai*). If you want to try this dish in Bangkok Gai ton Pratunam, is the place to go, as it has a solid reputation as the best khao man gai restaurant in the city. But you can find this dish almost everywhere, just look out for cooked chickens, mostly hanging up on hooks, and a big, steaming cooking pot filled with fragrant bouillon. There is also a version of this dish that uses duck instead of chicken (khao na pet), and if is duck you are looking for, try pet tun jao, where at least sixty ducks are sold every day.

It is in the evenings when, when Yawalat is lit up by countless colourful neon lights, and the streets are full of people cooking and eating, that I enjoy visiting Chinatown the most. The woks are working at full tilt and the sweet fragrance of frying garlic makes many a hungry man's mouth water as he joins those waiting at a favourite food stand. It is not unusual to see a shiny new Mercedes double-parked while the owner waits for his 20 baht pot of noodle soup.
You will find an abundance of seafood and fish in Chinatown: large langoustines, clams, salty oysters, meaty crabs, mussels and a vast array of fish, and everything as fresh as it could possibly be! Back home I dream of that kind of quality and quantity ...

T&K Seafood on the corner of Soi Texas and Yawalat is where you should go if you are looking for classic Thai food culture, in a colourful setting. The distinctive green polo shirts worn by the personnel will help you

easily recognise this culinary paradise. The freshest of seafood is deliciously prepared, at affordable prices. You may have to join the queue but the wait is definitely worthwhile. And actually it never takes too long before the friendly manager manages to point you to you a table. My favourites at this restaurant are the barbecued giant prawns served with a spicy dressing (*naam jim thaleh*), **deep fried crab** (*poo jaa*), and the **clams with roasted chilli paste** (*hoi laai phat phrik pao*). And fans of hot and sour should definitely try the **steamed sea bass with lime dressing** (*pla ka pong nung manao*)!

For me, Chinatown in the morning is a totally different place. During my last stay discovering Yawalat was, for me, a revelation. A whole world of tradition and well-kept cooking secrets unfolded before me. I would even go as far as saying it was a truly magical revelation. If you go exploring Bangkok, you will invariably be rewarded with an unforgettable experience. Drinking in a traditional coffee shop where they filter the coffee through a stocking (café boran) that you have discovered for yourself, in one of the narrow alleyways around Yawalat; for breakfast look for a place serving the delicious, hearty **rice soup with pork ribs** (*khao tom*) or a food stall selling **steamed buns** (*salapao*). Or, find your way through the winding passageways to get your lunch at a khao kaeng stand, where you can try **pork in yellow curry with butternut squash** (*gaeng fug moo*) or enjoy some **panang curry with pork** (*panang moo*) served with rice, is the most authentic culinary expedition experience ever. Mingle with the people going to or coming back from work, breath in the relaxed atmosphere, mix with the locals, and you will find more often than not they will be eager to exchange a few words in Thai or English with you. These are the moments when you will truly experience the genuine atmosphere of street food culture. Close to the Giant Swing Monument is a man in a pick-up truck who is definitely worth going and seeking out. Every day for years he has been preparing his **stir-fried glass noodles** (*pat woon sen*). You should also try some **green mango and sweet fish sauce dressing** (*mamouang nam pla wan*) on busy Yawalat Road. Dare to experiment, explore and immerse yourself in the wondrous and illustrious world that is Chinatown.

Originally a specialty from the Chinese island of Hainan brought to Thailand with the many poor Chinese immigrants. They had to be inventive and economical. Therefore, nothing is wasted. The chicken legs are deep-fried. The carcass and neck are used to make a stock. The stock serves as liquid to cook the rice, to eat as a soup and is used in the accompanying sauce.

— **Boiling**
ต้ม

Chicken on rice
ข้าวมันไก่

khao man gai

It's easy to spot the boiled chickens hanging on a hook on display accompanied by a large rice pot. This dish smells delicious and the fragrant rice is astonishing. Most Thai dishes are shared but this is more a 'one person - one plate' example. The soup served with this dish is heartwarming and is a complete meal.

Chicken

1 whole chicken
4 l water
1 pinch of salt
1 pinch of pepper
8 garlic cloves
2 coriander roots, scraped and bruised
1 handful of coriander stalks
500 g rice
100 g sticky rice, soaked in warm water for at least 3 hours
4 tbsp. vegetable oil
1 pinch of salt
1 pinch of sugar

Soup

1 small green gourd, peeled, deseeded and diced
1 tbsp. light soy sauce
1 pinch of white pepper
1 tbsp. spring onion, chopped
1 tbsp. coriander leaves

>>

Wash and clean the chicken. Put it in a large pot, cover with water; add salt, pepper, 3 garlic cloves, coriander roots and stalks, turn on low heat and simmer for 30 minutes, skimming regularly. Turn off the heat and leave the chicken in the stock to cool. Remove the chicken, take off the skin and remove the bones. Keep the meat separate. Skim off excess fat and strain. Chop the rest of the garlic finely and set aside.

Combine the 2 types of rice, rinse well and drain. Heat oil in a large pan on medium heat, add garlic and fry until golden. Take out 1 teaspoon of the fried garlic and set aside on a paper towel. Add rice and keep stirring for a few minutes. Season this with salt and sugar. Ladle enough stock over the rice to cover it. Most Thai people don't measure rice and water; they just take enough water so that the water covering the rice is in between the first and the second joint of your index finger. Do the same with the stock. Stir well, cover with a lid and cook over a very low heat until the rice is cooked. This should take about 20 minutes. Add extra stock if needed. >>

Sauce	Bring the remaining stock back to the boil, add the
4 tbsp. chicken stock	green gourd and simmer for about 10 minutes. Add
4 tbsp. yellow bean paste	soy sauce, pepper, spring onion, coriander and the
1 tbsp. dark soy sauce	reserved fried garlic. Combine all the ingredients for
1 tbsp. ginger, chopped	the sauce and mix well.
1 tsp. sugar	Spoon some of the rice on a plate, slice the chicken
	and put it on top. Garnish with cucumber and coriander
For garnish	leaves. Serve with a bowl of soup and a small dish
½ cucumber, sliced	of sauce.
coriander leaves	

Deep-fried dressed crab

ปู+จ๋า

poo jaa

Crab is one of the many seafood treats we can sample in abundance in Thailand. Best savoured simply steamed but this variation is also a winner.

Ingredients

400 g crab meat or
6 fresh small crabs
2 garlic cloves, chopped
1 tbsp. coriander leaves, chopped
1 pinch of ground black pepper
200 g minced pork (or chicken to substitute)
1 shallot, chopped
1 stalk of spring onion, chopped
2 tbsp. fish sauce
1 tsp. sugar
2 eggs, lightly beaten
6 crab shells if using crab meat

For garnish

coriander leaves, chopped
1 large red chilli, julienned

— When you're using fresh crabs, boil quickly in salted water until cooked. The cooking time depends on the size of the crabs. Ask your fishmonger how long they need to be cooked. Remove the meat and keep the shells. Clean the shells.

— Combine garlic, coriander and pepper in a mixing bowl. Add pork, crabmeat, shallot, spring onion, fish sauce and sugar. Mix well. Divide the mixture over the shells.

— Steam for about 15 minutes. Set aside to cool. Dip the steamed crab in the beaten egg. Deep-fry on medium heat, meat side down, until golden. Be careful not to deep-fry too long or the filling will fall out. Remove and drain well.

— Garnish with coriander leaves and chilli. Serve with cucumber relish (*ar jard* see p. 203) or with sweet chilli dip (*naam jim gai yang* see p. 206).

◊ — **Stir-Frying**
ผัด

Clams with roasted chilli paste

หอยลายผัดพริกเผา

hoi laai phat phrik pao

Ingredients

300 g fresh clams, soaked in
salted water for a few hours
to remove sand
2 tbsp. vegetable oil
2 garlic cloves, chopped finely
1 tbsp. fish sauce
1 tsp. sugar
2 tbsp. roasted chilli paste
1 large red chilli, sliced diagonally
2 handful of Thai basil

Put the wok on medium to high heat. When warm, add oil. Add garlic and clams. Stir-fry till the clams open. Add fish sauce, sugar and chilli paste and stir. Add chilli and Thai basil and stir.

◊ — *Steaming*
นึ่ง

Steamed sea bass with lime dressing

ปลากะพงขาวนึ่งมะนาว

pla ka pong nung manao

This is Eva's favourite! The fresh taste of the fish, the spicy-sour dressing, it all combines into a perfect, pure dish. And it's so easy to make!

Fish

1 whole sea bass or
400 g white fish fillet
2 stalks of lemon grass, bruised
4 kaffir lime leaves
6 slices galangal
1 coriander root, scraped and bruised
1 pinch of salt

Dressing

2 tbsp. coriander root, chopped
2 tbsp. garlic cloves, chopped
1 large red chilli, deseeded and chopped finely
5–20 small chillies, chopped
3 tbsp. fish sauce
4 tbsp. lime juice
1 tbsp. sugar
1 pinch of salt

For garnish

1 lime, sliced thinly
1 Chinese celery, chopped

Scatter lemon grass, kaffir lime leaves, galangal and coriander root on a plate. Put the fish on top and season with some salt. Steam this for about 15 minutes, depending on the size of the fish until cooked. Combine all ingredients for the dressing and mix well. When the fish is cooked, place the fish on a serving plate, spoon over some of the cooking liquid. Pour over the dressing, garnish with a few slices of lime and Chinese celery and serve immediately.

Sometimes the fish is half-steamed served in a bowl, shaped like a fish. Under this tray are burning charcoals so the fish can steam further when already served on the table.

: — **Boiling**
ต้ม

Rice soup with pork ribs

ข้าวต้มกระดูกซี่โครงหมู

khao tom kra dook moo

A bowl of rice soup for breakfast gives you a real energy boost.
A great start to the day!

Ingredients

600 g pork ribs, in 3 cm pieces
2 l water
2 tbsp. light soy sauce
2 tbsp. fish sauce
2 tbsp. oyster sauce
1 tbsp. sugar
½ tbsp. preserved radish or preserved cabbage, finely chopped
3 spring onions, chopped in rings
1 handful Chinese celery leaves
1 handful coriander leaves
1 tbsp. white pepper corns
500 g cooked rice
1 tbsp. fried garlic

Rinse the pork ribs under cold running water until they are completely cleaned. Put the 2 litres of water into a large pan and add the pork ribs. Bring gently to the boil and then allow to simmer over a low heat for an hour until the meat is tender.

Season the cooking liquid with the soy sauce, fish sauce, oyster sauce and sugar. Add the preserved radish, spring onion, Chinese celery and coriander leaves, and half of the white pepper.

Divide the rice into the serving dishes, and pour in the soup. Garnish with the fried garlic and remaining white pepper. The dish can also be served with Thai doughnuts (pa thong ko – see p. 42).

This dish can also be made equally successfully, substituting chicken or prawns for the pork.

 — **Steaming**
นึ่ง

Steamed bun
ซาลาเปา

salapao

This is originally a Chinese breakfast. Even Thai people call it
in English 'Chinese buns'. Variations of the fillings are possible.
You can use red barbecued pork, black beans, etc.

Makes 15 pieces

240 ml water
2 tbsp. vegetable oil
1 tbsp. sugar
1 tsp. salt
300 g wheat flour
½ tbsp fresh yeast

Filling

2 tbsp. vegetable oil
2 shallots, chopped
1 spring onion, chopped
200 g minced pork
1 tsp. ginger
3 tbsp. soy sauce
½ tsp. ground white pepper
½ tsp. sugar
4 tbsp. water
1 tsp. sesame oil

greaseproof paper
1 squirt of vinegar

First make the filling. Put vegetable oil in a wok,
stir-fry shallot, spring onion and pork for a few
minutes, until cooked. Add ginger, soy sauce, white
pepper, sugar and water. Keep simmering until all
the water is evaporated, and then add sesame oil.
Set aside and leave for 2 hours to cool and thicken.
For the dough, combine water, oil, sugar and salt
in a mixing bowl. Mix thoroughly. In a larger mixing
bowl, combine flour with yeast and pour in the
prepared mixture. Knead until the dough is firm.
Cover and leave to rise for 30 minutes at room
temperature.
Divide the dough into about 15 balls. Cut grease-
proof paper into 15 squares. Roll each ball flat.
Add a little oil if the dough sticks too much.
Scoop 1 teaspoon of the filling and place in middle
of disc, fold all sides in. Form a bun shape.
Place each bun on a square of grease-proof paper
in a steamer. Add a squirt of vinegar to the water
used for steaming; this will help to keep the buns
white. Steam the buns for about 10 minutes.

When leaving a 7-Eleven-store you might hear employees saying
ao salapao porm mai krap/ka. Do you want anything else?
Here 'anything else' is expressed by *salapao.*

:Ò: — **Boiling**
ต้ม

Pork in yellow curry with butternut squash
แกงฟักหมู
gaeng fug moo

The sweet taste of the pork is complemented with
the bitterness of the butternut squash.

Ingredients

200 g butternut squash,
in 3 cm cubes
1 tbsp. flour
300 g pork filet, in strips
225 ml thick coconut cream
(the thick layer from the top
of a can of coconut milk)
1 tbsp. yellow curry paste
2 tbsp. fish sauce
1 tbsp. sugar
400 ml coconut milk

Boil the butternut squash, for 20 minutes and drain.

Coat the pork strips in the flour and allow to rest in the fridge for 30 minutes.

Warm a wok over medium heat and add the thick coconut cream, then turn up the heat until the oil and coconut separate. Turn the heat down to low again, add the curry paste and cook through until the aromas are released and then season with the fish sauce and sugar.

Add the pork and cook until browned.

Add the coconut milk and bring gently to the boil. If desired add a little extra fish sauce for flavour. Serve with the cooked butternut squash, rice and cucumber relish (see p. 203).

☼ — **Stir-Frying**
ผัด

Curry paste: dry ingredients

2 tsp. coriander seeds (toasted)
½ tsp. cumin seeds (toasted)
½ whole nutmeg (toasted)
2 cardamom pods (toasted)
½ tsp. black pepper corns
½ tsp. salt
3 long green chilli peppers (toasted)
12 large dried red chillies
finely chopped (seeds removed,
soaked for 10 minutes in water)

Curry paste: fresh ingredients

1 tsp. finely chopped Laos ginger
2 tsp. finely chopped lemongrass
1 tsp. grated kaffir lime peel
1 tbsp. finely chopped coriander root
3 tbsp. finely chopped shallot
2 tbsp. finely chopped garlic
1 tsp. shrimp paste, toasted
2 to 3 tbsp. peanuts (first roasted
in the oven for about 30 minutes,
and then allowed to cool)

4 tbsp. thick coconut cream
(the thick layer from the top
of a can of coconut milk)
2 tbsp. curry paste (as above)
1 tbsp. fish sauce
1 tbsp. palm sugar
250 g pork loin, sliced into strips
1 handful small Thai aubergines
(stalks removed)
1 large fresh red chilli,
sliced diagonally into rings
200 ml coconut milk
5 kaffir lime leaves, vein removed and
chopped into very fine strips
1 handful Thai basil leaves

Panang curry with pork

พะแนงหมู

panang moo

One of my absolute favourite curries! Making your own curry paste is not only fun to do but the quality is guaranteed, with no flavour enhancers or additives. The use of finely chopped peanuts and nutmeg in the curry paste gives it a sweeter taste. Panang is creamy but dryer and milder than red curry.

Begin by making the curry paste, first grind the dry ingredients together in a pestle and mortar, then add in the fresh ingredients and combine until a smooth paste has formed, keep to one side.

Warm the wok over a high heat. Put in the coconut cream and break up until the fat separates to the top.

Turn the heat down as low as possible and add the curry paste. Allow to cook gently for 2 minutes without stirring. If the paste starts sticking to the pan add a little vegetable oil to prevent it burning.

Season the curry paste mix to taste, with the fish sauce and palm sugar, and mix well. Add the pork and stir-fry until the meat is nicely browned. Now add in the aubergines and the chilli and continue to stir-fry for 1 more minute.

Pour in the coconut milk and bring to the boil. Finally add the kaffir leaves and the Thai basil. Serve with rice.

 — **Stir-Frying**
ผัด

Stir-fried glass noodles with seafood

ผัดวุ้นเส้น

phat woon sen

Glass noodles are the perfect accompaniment to seafood.

Ingredients

200 g minced pork
2 tbsp. fish sauce
1 tsp. sugar
1 tbsp. ground tapioca
oil for frying
2 bundles glass noodles
2 tbsp. vegetable oil
1 garlic clove, crushed
2 eggs
8 scampi, peeled and cleaned
1 squid body, cut into rings
1 tbsp. light soy sauce
1 handful Chinese celery leaves
salad leaves

First make the pork patties. Mix the pork mince with 1 tablespoon of the fish sauce, half a teaspoon of the sugar and the ground tapioca and form into small patties about 5 cm in diameter. Pre-heat the oil and fry the pork patties for a few minutes on each side until golden brown. Keep to one side.

Cook the glass noodles in water according to the packet instructions. Drain.

Put the vegetable oil into a wok and add in the crushed garlic. Add the eggs and stir-fry until they firm up. Move the egg to the edge of the wok. Add the scampi and cook for one minute then add the squid rings and stir-fry for a further minute. Add the noodles to the wok and bring the egg back into the centre of the wok and thoroughly combine. Now add the remaining fish sauce, soy sauce and sugar and if needed, a little extra water. Finish with the Chinese celery leaves.

To serve; divide the salad leaves onto the serving plates followed by the noodle and seafood mixture. Finish by laying the pork patties on top.

Green mango and sweet fish sauce dressing

มะม่วงน้ำปลาหวาน

mamouang nam pla wan

I had to get used to the idea of fish and fruit at first,
but now I think it is delicious.

Ingredients

80 ml fish sauce
1 tsp. shrimp paste
150 g palm sugar
50 g dried shrimp
1 sour green mango, grated
3 shallots cut lengthways into strips
4 bird's eye chillies,
sliced into fine rings

Warm the fish sauce with the shrimp paste and the palm sugar over a low heat until the sugar has dissolved then remove from the heat. The syrup will thicken slightly as it cools.

Place half of the dried shrimp into a mortar and grind to a powder. Mix the shallot and the other half of the dried shrimp into the syrup mixture, and then add the chillies and the ground dried shrimp powder.

Grate the green mango into shreds and combine with the dressing to serve.

If you can't find green mango, green Granny Smith apples are a good alternative.

Tradition and renewal

Just before I boarded my Thai Airways flight from Brussels to Bangkok, I began reading *Bangkok found*, an interesting and well researched book by Alex Kerr. Half-way through is a passage that touched me deeply. Alex describes a conversation with his friend Tom Vitayakul and their discussion of the origins of Thai cuisine. With great passion he analyses the ingredients of the green papaya salad, a very common street snack from the North East. Bird's eye chilli, lime, tomatoes, and papaya are the four basic ingredients and all of them foreign, leaving only the fish sauce as an authentic Thai ingredient. This to me is yet another indication that Thai cuisine, just as Thai society has always been accepting and greatly influenced by other parts of the world, adapting to and absorbing new ideas. And this openness of spirit and acceptance of other cultures is definitely a recognisable character trait of Thai society as a whole.

On the last day of our stay we met up with two friends who were visiting Thailand for the first time and were just beginning their journey. Inevitably we ended up going out for a few Leo beers on a street in the Khao San neighbourhood and we were astonished by how much this area has changed in recent years. We started with a **fermented tea leaf salad** (*lapet thoke*). Originating in Burma this creation is the most unusual taste sensation I have had the pleasure of trying for years. We moved on to Krua Apsorn, a restaurant that is a bit further north on the Samsen Road. I treated Erwin, Geert and Luk to a few words of wisdom, introducing them to the basics of Thai cuisine and also to a **mushroom salad** (*laab het*) and a **sour curry with tiger prawns and lotus stems** (*gaeng som*) with **fishcakes** (*thod man pla*) as an aperitif.

We first published *Bangkok street food; cooking and travelling in Thailand* in 2009. At about the same time David Thompson's book *Thai street food*, was also released; a richly illustrated masterpiece about Thai street food culture. At the time the term Street food was still only vaguely understood, and I don't think that it is a title the Thai street cooks would have recognised then, and probably never will.

Ten years ago, it was difficult to find any useful information about street food in Bangkok, in English. However, thanks to food bloggers and street food addicts like Marc Wiens, today there is a treasure trove of information available on the internet. This points not only to the increase in interest on the subject but also ensures an exchange of knowledge whereby dishes become more accessible and available and therefore have a greater chance of surviving for future generations.

Though fundamentally little has changed in the last ten years, street food in Thailand has become maybe just a little more commercialised. There are new additions to the scene such as the farmers' or organic markets, travel companies organised excursions, and the descriptive menus that hang on boards in Sam Phraeng. There are also the trendy food trucks selling hamburgers, hot dogs and 'Belgiamese' waffles, new trends which we can only applaud; it doesn't matter if it is traditional or not. It gives me great pleasure to see areas such as Sam Phraeng and Chinatown doing their best to protect and keep their street food heritage alive, but at the same time I am buoyed up by the fun, new, hip street food concepts. In the city of Bangkok old and new, tradition and the latest trends have always gone hand in hand.

According to the United Nations more than two billion people eat street food every day. This does not merely provide a source of energy and nutrition, but for many also employment. Street food is therefore maybe the most important and biggest food industry in the world. Meanwhile street food is also becoming a trend in the west, and is resonating through the gourmet world. Well-equipped and beautifully styled food trucks, well thought out street food concepts and street food festivals now belong to and have become permanent fixtures in the culinary portfolio. Street food has in the last decade grown into a commercially important and global concept.

The authenticity of the dishes served is not always strictly adhered to; and without doubt there is a certain amount of standardisation. It is however equally important that street food gets the recognition it rightly deserves. We need to support the evolution of street food; economically, socially, environmentally and publicly. After all there is no better way of uniting people, than by sharing the same food.

Fermented tea leaf salad
ยำใบชาหมัก
yum bai cha muck (laphet thoke)

Absolutely one of the most surprising taste sensations of recent years, it is impossible to do justice to this dish in words.

Salad

200 g fermented tea leaves
2 tbsp. toasted sesame seeds
2 tbsp. roasted peanuts,
finely ground
2 tbsp. toasted dried soya beans,
finely ground
1 tbsp. toasted sticky rice finely ground
2 tomatoes, chopped
¼ Chinese cabbage, finely chopped

Dressing

¼ tsp. sugar
2 bird's eye chillies,
copped into fine rings
3 tbsp. lime juice
2 tbsp. fish sauce

In a mixing bowl combine the salad ingredients thoroughly with your hands. Combine the dressing ingredients; the sugar, chillies lime juice and fish sauce and add to the salad ingredients. Thoroughly mix again and serve immediately.

Laphet thoke is the national dish of Burma, or as it is now called, Myanmar. Because of the large number of Burmese immigrants in Bangkok it has also become popular in Thailand.

🔥 — **Boiling**
ต้ม

Mushroom salad

ลาบ เห็ด

laab het

This salad originates from Isaan, the north east region
of Thailand; a delicious vegetarian side dish.

Ingredients

200 ml water
200 g mixed mushrooms
1 tsp. chilli powder
2 spring onions, coarsely chopped
2 shallots cut into rings
3 tbsp. lime juice
2 tbsp. light soy sauce
½ tsp. sugar
1 tbsp. toasted sticky rice, finely ground.
1 handful mint leaves
1 handful coriander leaves
lettuce leaves (to serve)

Put the water into a saucepan and bring to the boil. Add the mushrooms and cook until tender (no more than 5 minutes).

Remove the mushrooms and place into a mixing bowl. Add the chilli powder, spring onions and shallot, and combine thoroughly.

Dress with the lime juice, soy sauce and sugar, coating the salad well. Add the ground rice powder and mix again. Finally add in the herbs and serve on a lettuce leaf.

♨ — **Boiling**
ต้ม

Sour curry with tiger prawns and lotus stems

แกงส้มกุ้ง

gaeng som kung

Perhaps the most 'Thai' of all Thai curries. With complex flavours and a really good balance of sour, sweet and savoury notes.

Tiger prawns and lotus stems

300 g unpeeled tiger prawns
1 l water
4 tbsp. tamarind paste, squeezed out in 100 ml warm water
2 tbsp. palm sugar
1 or 2 tbsp. fish sauce
120 g lotus stems, cut into 3cm pieces

Curry paste

4 large dried chillies, seeds removed, finely chopped
4 large fresh chillies, seeds removed, finely chopped
50 g krachai ginger, finely chopped
3 shallots, roughly chopped
1 tsp. shrimp paste
3 prawns, finely chopped
1 tsp. sea salt

Grind all the ingredients for the curry paste together to form a smooth paste.

Bring the water to the boil then add the unpeeled tiger prawns to the water.

Remove after 1 minute, or just before they are cooked through, but reserve the cooking liquid. Add in the curry paste and allow to cook through for about 5 minutes. Season the curry to taste with the sugar and fish sauce.

Add the lotus stems and cook for another five minutes until they are soft.

Add the tiger prawns back in to the sauce and cook for 1 more minute, then serve with rice.

This is a very cheap and filling snack.
You receive it in a small plastic bag with
a bamboo stick. Indicate if you want
some dressing poured over it.

— Deep-Frying
ทอด

Fishcakes
ทอดมันปลา
thod man pla

You will see a lot of food vendors deep-frying these little delicacies.
It's amazing to see them puff up. Eat them while they are still hot,
they toughen up as they cool.

Ingredients
300 g white fish fillets, chopped finely
4 tbsp. red curry paste
3 tbsp. fish sauce
1 egg, lightly beaten
1 tbsp. palm sugar or granulated sugar
5 kaffir lime leaves, deveined and shredded
2 tbsp. finely cut snake beans or green beans
oil for deep-frying

Put all ingredients into a mixing bowl. Mix thoroughly (either use your hands, a pestle and mortar or a food processor) until you get a smooth paste.
Take a large bowl, gather the paste together and throw it into the bowl. Continue this process until the mixture is firm. Doing this makes the fishcakes not puff up when deep-fried.
Divide in small portions and make small discs. Deep-fry until golden, drain and serve immediately with the cucumber relish (*ar jard*, see p. 203).

You can vary the recipe by substituting prawns, crab or even chicken, for the fish. The ready-made curry paste is available in most Thai food shops.

Thai language is peppered with hundreds of proverbs regarding food, more evidence of their passion and commitment to food. *Nuad* is the Thai word for massage. That's exactly what they call the throwing of the fishcake to make it more firm. Massaging fish cake!

201

Sauces, dips and pastes

As most sauces, dressings and pastes are prepared beforehand, we are putting these in a separate section. The thing that distinguishes so many dishes world-wide, after all is often the subtlety of the sauce or dressing. You can easily become proficient in the basic cooking techniques but if you truly want to master a cuisine you must also know how to give that added note of authenticity to your cooking. Without the particular dip or dressing that goes with the dish, you are missing a part of the true Thai taste experience.

Cucumber relish

อาจาด

ar jard

This is a refreshing accompaniment; it works especially well with fish cakes. You can also add julienned ginger or coarsely chopped roasted peanuts if you want.

Ingredients

4 tbsp. water
3 tbsp. sugar
3 tbsp. vinegar
1 pinch of salt
½ tsp. chilli powder or 1 large red
    chilli, julienned
4 tbsp. cucumber, julienned
2 tbsp. shallot, sliced
1 tbsp. coriander leaves, chopped

- Bring water with sugar, vinegar and salt to the boil.
- Turn off the heat when sugar has dissolved. Cool.
- Add chilli, cucumber and shallot.
- Finish with coriander leaves.

Fish sauce and chilli

น้ำปลาพริก

naam pla phrik

This dressing is quintessentially Thai. It's the Thai equivalent of our pepper & salt, combined in one bowl. Mostly served with rice dishes but then again, a lot of dishes come with rice in Thailand.

Ingredients

3-5 medium chillies,
    sliced finely in rings
1 garlic clove, chopped finely
5 tbsp. fish sauce
1 tbsp. lime juice

- Mix all the ingredients.

Peanut sauce

น้ำจิ้มสะเต๊ะ
naam satay

น้ำจิ้มถั่ว
naam jim thua

Ingredients
2 large dried chillies, chopped
2 garlic cloves, chopped
1 stalk lemongrass, chopped
1 tbsp. turmeric, chopped
2 tbsp. vegetable oil
450 ml coconut milk
1 tbsp. tamarind water
2 tbsp. sugar
½ tsp. salt
8 tbsp. ground roasted peanuts

Pound the chilli, garlic, lemongrass and turmeric in a mortar until smooth.

Heat oil in a wok on a low heat and fry the paste until fragrant.

Add coconut milk and bring to the boil. Keep boiling for 7 minutes.

Add tamarind water, sugar, salt and peanuts. Keep on boiling for 5 minutes.

Chilli powder dip from the Isaan

น้ำจิ้มแจ่ว
naam jim jaew

Ingredients
8 tbsp. lime juice
2 tbsp. fish sauce
½ tbsp. oyster sauce
1 tbsp. chilli powder
1 tbsp. toasted sticky rice, ground
1 shallot, sliced finely
2 tbsp. coriander leaves and stalks, chopped

Mix all the ingredients well.

Chilli paste
น้ำพริกเผา
naam phrik pao

The 'magic sauce' according to our dear friend Pi Toon and we can only, as always, agree with her.

Ingredients

oil for deep-frying
15 shallots, sliced
8 garlic cloves, sliced
8 tbsp. dried shrimp, rinsed and dried
8 tbsp. dried large red chillies, deseeded and chopped
10 slices galangal
1 tsp. shrimp paste, roasted
10 tbsp. palm sugar, chopped
8 tbsp. thick tamarind water
6 tbsp. fish sauce

Heat the oil in a wok and deep-fry one by one the shallots, garlic, dried shrimp, chillies and galangal. Drain on a paper towel. Blend them all in a food processor. Add the shrimp paste, blend. Moisten with some oil used for deep-frying, up to 16 tablespoons, to smooth the progress of the blending.

Bring the mixture to the boil in a pan. Season with palm sugar, tamarind water and fish sauce. Simmer and stir regularly until it has a thick jam like consistency. It should taste sweet, sour and salty. Adjust the seasoning if necessary.

Phrik pao works amazingly well with seafood of any kind. Sometimes it's used as a dip sauce. It is essential in a *tom yam kung*.

Sweet chilli dip
น้ำจิ้มไก่ย่าง
naam jim gai yang

The Thai name is somewhat misleading, as it literally means 'dip for grilled chicken'. Don't worry, it can be served with plenty of other dishes.

Ingredients

7 large, red chillies, deseeded and chopped

2 garlic cloves, chopped

12 tbsp. vinegar

8 tbsp. sugar

½ tsp. salt

Pound the chillies and garlic in a mortar until smooth.
Bring vinegar, sugar and salt to the boil.
Stir until sugar has dissolved.
Turn down the heat to medium.
Add chilli paste and simmer until it has a syrup-like consistency.

Spicy seafood dip
น้ำจิ้มทะเล
naam jim thaleh

Ingredients

5 garlic cloves, chopped

4-6 small green chillies, chopped

5 tbsp. lime juice

4 tbsp. fish sauce

1 tsp. sugar

2 tbsp. coriander leaves, chopped (optional)

Pound the garlic and chillies in a mortar until smooth.
Add lime juice, fish sauce and sugar and mix well until sugar has dissolved.
Add coriander leaves if using.

Shrimp paste relish
น้ำพริกกะปิ
naam phrik kapi

Ingredients

4 garlic cloves, peeled
1 pinch of salt
1 tbsp. shrimp paste, roasted
4-5 small chillies
1 tbsp. palm sugar
1 tbsp. lime juice
1 tsp. fish sauce
water if necessary

Pound garlic, salt and shrimp paste in a mortar until smooth. Add chillies. If you want a fiery dip, pound more until the chillies are pulverised. Season with palm sugar, lime juice and fish sauce. You may want to dilute it with some water. Just add one spoonful at a time, the consistency should be a slightly watery paste. Garnish with red chillies and small egg plants.

This is a basic version of this relish; there are probably as many versions as there are taxis in Bangkok. You can add pea-sized Thai eggplant *makheua phuang* if you can find it in your store. Or add coriander root, kaffir lime leaves to your paste. Try it and see for yourself what you like. It should always taste rich, salty, hot and sour though.

207

Thai language

Thai is a tonal language and thus extremely difficult to learn. Five diffe-rent tones are used: low (à), middle, high (á), falling (â) and rising (ā). The meaning of a single syllable can be altered in fi ve different ways. Here is an example with four tones and one syllable: *mái mài mâi māi*, means 'new word burns, doesn't it'. In our experience, the right word in the wrong tone is not understood or 'automatically corrected' by Thai people. This can lead to hilarious or frustrating experiences, depending on your attitude. Be pa-tient, remember that you are the tourist, you are visiting them. Sometimes a lot of gesticulation can also be a way of communicating.

However, if you do make an effort, you will notice that a few words of Thai vocabulary will make a difference! In the cities English is widely spoken, but if you really want to discover hidden gems, try to master some Thai. You will be rewarded with excellent treats!

Important: if you're a man, you should end your sentence with *khráp*. Women use *khâ*. There is not a literal translation but these syllables expresses politeness.

English	Phonetic Thai	Thai
Hello	*Sawàt dee*	สวัสดี
How are you	*Sàbai dee mãi*	สบายดีไหม
I'm fine	*Sàbai dee*	สบายดี
Thank you	*Khòp khun*	ขอบคุณ
Good luck/cheers	*Chôk dee*	โชคดี่
No problem/it's ok/ never mind	*Mâi pen rai*	ไม่เป็นไร
I understand	*Khâo jai*	เข้าใจ
I don't understand	*Mâi khâo jai*	ไม่เขาใจ
This, here	*Têe nêe*	ที่นี่
There	*Têe nân*	ที่นั่น
Over there	*Têe nôhn*	ที่โน่น
What	*Àrai*	อะไร
How much is...?	*Tâo rài*	เท่าไหร่
Do you have...?	*Mii ... mãi*	มี... ไหม
Can I...?	*Dâai ... mãi*	ได้... ไหม
I would like to...	*Yàak jà ...*	อยากจะ...
I like...	*Châwp ...*	ชอบ...
To eat	*Kin khâo*	กินข้าว
Good	*Dee*	ดี
Bad	*Mâi dee*	ไม่ดี
Delicious	*Àroî*	อร่อย
Difficult	*Yâak*	ยาก
Easy	*Mâi yâak*	ไม่ยาก
Spicy	*Pèt*	เผ็ด

On the map

Addresses

1 Chiang Mai curry noodles with chicken > *p. 39*
khao soi gai
Khao soi Chang Mai Suparp
283, Samsen Road, Phra Nathon
Bangkok
Open: 09:00 – 16:00, closed on Saturday

2 Green papaya salad > *p. 68*
som tam
Namtok Sida
Wang Lang market
112/5-6 Soi Wang Lang, Arun Amarin Road
Bangkok
Open: 09:00 – 19:00, closed on Sunday

3 Coconut with green chendol jelly beans > *p. 86*
lod chung Singapore
Singapore Pochana
680 – 682, Charoen Krung Road
Bangkok
Open: 11:00 – 22:00, every day

4 Rolled noodles with pork > *p. 91*
kuay chap nam sai
Kuay chap Nai Ek
442, Yaowaraj Road Soi 9
Bangkok
Open: 07:00 – 24:00, closed on Saturday

5 Stir-fried crab with yellow curry > *p. 114*
poo phat pong kari
Khao Tom Polo
137/14, Soi Sanam Khli (Soi Polo)
Bangkok
Open: 18:00 – 22:00, closed on Sunday

6 Braised goose in a brown gravy > *p. 116*
harn pra loh
Tang Hong Pochana (Harn pra loh Convent)
2/2, Soi Convent, Silom Road,
Bangkok
Open: 08:30 – 18:00, closed on Sunday

7 Oxtail soup > *p. 120*
soup hang wua
Muslim Restaurant
1354-56 (Soi 42), Charoen Krung
Bangkok
Open: 06:00 – 17:00, every day

8 Stir-fried noodles with pork and gravy
> *p. 122*
kuaytiaw raat na sai moo
Saeng Yod
74, Charat Wianbg Road, Silom, Bangrak
Bangkok
10:00 – 18:00, closed on Sunday

9 Crispy noodles > *p. 129*
mee khrob
Chote Chitr restaurant
146, Prang Pu Thorn
Bangkok
Open: (very irregular) 11:00 – 15:00,
closed on Sunday

10 Sweet sticky rice with coconut and mango
> *p. 136*
khap niaw mamuang
Kao Niaw Korpanich
430-431, Tanao Road
Bangkok
Open: 06:30 – 19:00, closed on Sunday

11 Crispy coconut pancakes with salty
or sweet topping > *p. 139*
khanom buang
Khanom Buang Phraeng Nara
Tanao Road
Bangkok
Open: 10:00 – 18:00, closed on Sunday

12 Coconut sorbet & Mango ice cream > *p. 142*
Natthapon Coconut Icecrem
94, Phraeng Phuton Road
Bangkok
Open: 09:00 – 17:00, every day

13 Grilled red pork > *p. 145*
moo deng
Udom Pochana
78, Phraeng Phutorn Road
Bangkok
Open: 07:30 – 15:30, closed on Sunday

14 Stir-fried rice with shrimp paste > *p. 149*
khao kluk kapi
Yong Seng Lee
Phra Nakhon
Bangkok
Open: 10:00 – 14:00, 17:00 – 19:00,
closed on Sunday

15 Stir-fried noodles with prawns > *p. 157*
phat thai
Thip Samai
313, Mahachai Road
Bangkok
Open: 18:00 – 24:00, every day

16 Chicken on rice > *p. 171*
khao man gai
Gai ton Pratunam
Petchaburi Road, Soi 30
Bangkok
Open: 18:00 – 02:00, every day

17 Steamed sea bass with lime dressing
> *p. 179*
pla ka pong nung manao
T & K seafood
49, 51, Phadung Dao Road (Soi Texas),
Yaowalaj Road
Bangkok
Open: 16:30 – 24:00, every day

18 Panang curry with pork > *p. 186*
Panang moo
Khao Kaeng Jek Pui (Jay Chia)
Thanon Mangkon
Bangkok
Open: 15:30 – 21:30

19 Green mango and sweet fish sauce
dressing > *p. 191*
mamouang nam pla wan
Mamuang Nam Pla Wan Jay Paew
Yaowaraj Road at the crossroad with
Plaeng Nam Road
Bangkok
Open: 09:00 – 24:00, every day

20 Sour curry with tiger prawns and
lotus stems > *p. 198*
gaeng som kung
Krua Apsorn
Samsen Road just past the *national library*
Bangkok
Open: 12:00 – 15:00 / 18:00 – 20:00
closed on Sunday

Markets

A **Thewet and the Thewet food market**
Open: 06:00 – 12:00
Pier Chao Phraya River Express boat:
Tha Thewez

B **Nang Loeng Market**
Open: 10:00 – 13:00, week days
Nakhon Sawan, opposite number 400

C **Amulet market**
Open: 10:00 – 17:00
Pier Chao Phraya River Express boat:
Tha Chang

D **Wang Lang market**
Open: 10:00 – 18:00
Next to the Siriraj Hospital
Pier Chao Phraya River Express boat:
Tha Wang Lang

E **Pak Khlong Talad**
Wholesale market with vegetables,
flowers and plants
Open: 04:00 – 10:00
Pier Chao Chao Phraya River Express
boat: Tha Rachani

F **Soachingcha-district**
Open: 06:00 – 18:00
Along the Tanao Road and Dinso Road
(between Ratchadamnoen, City hall & the
Giant Swing monument)

G **Sam Phraeng district**
Traditional dishes at various locations
throughout the neighbourhood
Open: 06:00 – 18:00
Area opposite the Kao Niaw Korpanich,
Tanao Road 430

H **Old Siam Plaza**
Open: 09:00 – 21:00
Burapha Road, Phranakorn,
close to Little India

I **Chinatown**
Open: 06:00 – 02:00
Yawalat Road, Charoeng Krung
and side streets

J **Banglampoo food market**
Open: 07:00 – 17:00, closed on Sunday
Thanon Chakhraphong 136-40

K **Silm Soi 20**
Open: 06:00 – 14:00
BTS station: Chong Nonsi

L **Sukhumvit Soi 38**
Open: 18:00 – 02:00
Sukhumvit Road Soi 38
BTS station: Tong Lo

M **Soi Ari**
Open: 18:00 – 22:00, week days
BTS station: Ari

N **Victory Monument**
Streets around the Victory monument
(North side)
Open: 08:00 – 19:00
BTS station: Victory monument

O **Or-Tor-Kor market**
Open: 06:00 – 18:00
Thanon Kamphaengphet
BTS station: Moi chit
MRT station: Chatuchak markt

P **Samyan market**
Open: 07:00 – 13:00
Soi Chulalongkorn 32 – 34
MRT station: Sam yan

Q **Klong Toey market**
Open: 06:00 – 21:00
Junction of Rama IV / Rama III Road
MRT station: Khlong Toey

Index

Colophon

With special thanks to my best friend Eva Verplaetse.

www.lannoo.com
Register on our website and we will regularly send you a newsletter with information about new books and exciting exclusive offers.

Text: Tom Vandenberghe, www.eetavontuur.be & www.eetramen.be
Photography and food styling: Luk Thys, www.foodphoto.be
Design: Klaartje De Buck, Letterwerf
Translation: Fran Oosterbaan-Clarke

Check out: www.ilikestreetfood.com

If you have observations or questions, please contact our editorial office: redactielifestyle@lannoo.com.

© Uitgeverij Lannoo nv, Tielt, 2015
D/2015/45/484 – NUR 442
ISBN: 978-94-014-2440-0